The RV Camping Bible

A Complete Guide to Make the Most of Your Life on the Road
Discover Secret Campsites, Memorable Outdoor Activities and Achieve Your Dream RV Experience

Eric Foster

© **Copyright 2023 - All rights reserved.**

The content contained within this book may not be reproduced, duplicated or transmitted without direct written permission from the author or the publisher.

Under no circumstances will any blame or legal responsibility be held against the publisher, or author, for any damages, reparation, or monetary loss due to the information contained within this book. Either directly or indirectly.

Legal Notice:

This book is copyright protected. This book is only for personal use. You cannot amend, distribute, sell, use, quote or paraphrase any part, or the content within this book, without the consent of the author or publisher.

Disclaimer Notice:

Please note the information contained within this document is for educational and entertainment purposes only. All effort has been executed to present accurate, up to date, and reliable, complete information. No warranties of any kind are declared or implied. Readers acknowledge that the author is not engaging in the rendering of legal, financial, medical or professional advice. The content within this book has been derived from various sources. Please consult a licensed professional before attempting any techniques outlined in this book.

By reading this document, the reader agrees that under no circumstances is the author responsible for any losses, direct or indirect, which are incurred as a result of the use of information contained within this document, including, but not limited to, — errors, omissions, or inaccuracies.

Table Of Contents

PART I – THE POWER OF MINIMALISM 8

INTRODUCTION 9

EMBRACING MINIMALISM 11
    How People Have Too Much Useless Stuff 11

MY APPROACH TO GETTING RID OF STUFF 14
    Downsizing for the Count 15
    A Downsizing Plan 15
    Items You Cannot Get Rid of 15
    Downsize Your Clothes 16
    Donate or Sell Your Clothes 16
    Trash Your Clothes 16
    Store Some Clothes 17
    Essential Kitchen Items to Take 17
    Kitchen Items to Donate or Sell 18
    Essential Bedding/Sofa Items to Take 18
    Bedding Items to Donate or Sell 19
    Bedding Items to Store 19
    Documents to Keep in the RV 19

EVALUATING FUTURE PURCHASE 20
    Where Things Could Turn Sour 20

MYTHS TO DEBUNK 22

PART II – TIPS FOR BUYING AN RV 27

CHOOSING THE RIGHT RV FOR YOU 28
    Points to Remember Before Buying an RV 28
    Types of RVs 31

HOW TO BUY AN RV? 36
    Select Your RV 36
    Find a Dealer 36
    Negotiate the Price 36
    Checklist for Inspection 37
    Collect the Documents 38

WHY YOU SHOULD NEVER BUY A BRAND-NEW RV 39

PART III – RV DRIVING & TESTING 43

HOW TO LEARN TO DRIVE YOUR RV 44
    In a Nutshell, Here's How to Drive an RV 44
    How to Turn to the Right 44
    How to Turn to the Left 45
    Walmart Can Help You Learn to Drive 45
    Backing Your RV 46
    More Points about Driving 47
    An RV Driving Course Manual 47
    Sign Up for an RV Driving Course 47

- Licensing 48
- Plan Ahead 48

HOW TO TEST YOUR RV 49
- Exterior 49
- Interior 49
- Road Test 50

PART IV – PROS, CONS, AND ESSENTIAL TIPS 51

HOW MUCH DOES RV LIVING COST? 52
- The Financial Questions You'll Need to Ask Are 52
- RV Hosting Websites 53
- How About Cell Phone and Internet Service? 54
- What Will I Spend on Laundry? 54
- Entertainment—How Much Fun Money? 54
- Groceries, Clothes, Etc. 54

DECORATING AN RV 56
- The Most Efficient Method to Design an RV 56
- Improve an RV 56
- Envision a Completed RV 56
- Time to Brighten an RV 57
- Cherishing Your RV 57

THE PROS AND CONS OF FULL-TIME RVING 58
- Cons 58
- Pros 59

TRANSITIONING INTO THE RV LIFESTYLE 61
- Adjusting to Your New Life on the Road 61
- How to Survive Living in a Small Space? 62
- Traveling with Kids and Animals 63
- Tips for RVing with Your Kids 63
- Tips for RVing with Pets 64
- Making Your RV Feel Like Home 65

WHAT YOU NEED TO KNOW BEFORE YOU GO 67
- How Do You Dump the Tanks? 67
- Types of RV Tanks 67
- Regular Maintenance on the Road 68
- What to Do If the RV Breaks Down 70
- When Trouble Comes Knocking at the Door 70
- Electricity and Power 70

PART V – BOONDOCKING 101 72

CAMPING AND BOONDOCKING BASICS 73
- Campsites for Your RV 73
- Urban Camping 74
- Boondocking 75
- RV Clubs and Memberships 77
- The Best RV Club Memberships 77

FACTORS THAT AFFECT RV AND CAMPING 80
- Pandemics 80
- About Crowding 80
- RV Sizes 81

SURVIVAL TIPS AND STAYING SAFE WHILE BOONDOCKING 82
Basic Survival Tips for Boondocking 83
Dealing with Insects and Animals While Boondocking 85

PART VI – THE EMOTIONAL SIDE OF RV LIVING 87

EMOTIONAL ASPECTS OF RVING 88
Major Emotional Concerns 88
Problems Will Arise 89
Living in an RV Won't Fix All the Problems in Your Life 90

WHY DO YOU WANT TO LIVE IN AN RV? 92
What Is the Housing Situation in California? 92
The Benefits of a Ranger 92

IS FEAR HOLDING YOU BACK? 95
Fear Shows Up in Many Forms 95
The Risk of Change 98

SOLO RVING DONE RIGHT 100
Solo RVing Tips 100
If You Follow These Simple Tips, You'll Be Fine on the Road! 101

PART VII – HEALTH, KITCHEN ORGANIZATION, AND SAFETY TIPS 105

STOCKING YOUR RV VEHICLE 106
Stocking in the Optional Essentials 106
Your Vacation Budget 107
RV Rentals 107
How Can You Rent? 107
How to Get the Best Rental Rate? 108

FOOD AND STAYING HEALTHY 109
Stocking Food 109
Food Preparation 110
Cooking Methods on the Road 110
Staying Healthy and Clean 111
Health Care on the Road 112

OUTDOOR KITCHEN ORGANIZATION TIPS, TRICKS, AND ESSENTIAL ITEMS 113
There Are Many Advantages to Making All Meals Outside 113

SAFETY – WHAT PRECAUTIONS YOU NEED TO TAKE 117
Personal Safety 117
RV Safety 118

PART VIII – RV PROBLEMS, MAINTENANCE, AND TRAVEL TIPS 119

COMMON RV PROBLEMS AND SOLUTIONS 120
Driving Into Overhead Obstructions 120
Tire Blowouts 121
Battery Failure 121
Toilet Issues 121

RV MAINTENANCE 123
DIY and Preventative Support 123
Standard Adjusting and Upkeep 124
A Snappy Word on Dumping 124

WHAT TO KNOW AND WHERE TO GO 127
Choosing a Destination 127
How to Get There 128
While You Are Traveling 128

MAKING MONEY ON THE ROAD 130
Seasonal Employment 130
Camp Site Work: Also Known as "Workamping" 131
Artisan Items 132
Using Your Own Set Skills 133
Working Online 133
Online Auction Sites 133

PART IX – RV LIFE HACKS: STAYING CONNECTED, AND FAQS 135

STAYING CONNECTED 136
Millennials Have It Made 136
DIY Photojournalism 137

DOMICILE, MAIL, VOTING, BANKING, AND TAXES 140
Choosing Your State of Domicile 140
RV Terms to Know 140
Factors to Think About 141
Where Should Your Domicile Be? 142
Taxes: Sales, Income, and Property 143
Other Factors: Insurance, Education, Ease, and Ethics 144

WINTERIZING AND DE-WINTERIZING YOUR RV 145
Winterizing 145
De-Winterizing 146

GADGETS 148
Air Lounger 148
Folding Bikes 148
Smart Space Heaters 149
Nested Cookware 149
Mini Torch 149
Instant Pot 150
Folding Firepit 150
Foldable Luggage or Travel Bags 150

MY FAVORITE SPOTS TRAVEL GUIDE 152

COMMONLY ASKED QUESTIONS 154
What Is the Worst Thing About Living in an RV? 154
What Is the Best Thing About RV Life? 154
How Can You Do Laundry? 154
Do You Feel Safe on The Road? 154
Isn't Gas Mileage Terrible? 155
When Will You Start Living a Normal Life Again? 155
Can You RV Full-Time in the Winter? 155
How Do You Stay in Shape While on the Road? 155
Do You Get Tired of Living in a Small Space? 155
What Do You Do with the Poop? 156
Do You Need a Special License to Drive a Motorhome? 156
How Do You Cook Meals? 156
Where Do You Stay When the RV Needs Service? 156

CONCLUSION 157
#1: Prepare Your Mind 157
#2: Prepare Your Body 157
#3: Prepare Your Finances 157
#4: Prepare Your Time 158
#5: Prepare Your Life Partner—Marriage or Cohabitation 158

Part I

—

The Power of Minimalism

Introduction

RV living can seem complicated and overwhelming for the uninitiated. Most people assume that living in an RV requires a lot of understanding about how it works, including all the different features are, how you stop or start it, and so on. But this book is going to show you just how easy-peasy RV living can be for beginners."

What do you need to know about making your life more accommodating? As flexible as taking off from one place and soaring down another with no regard for the location or personal space? Here are some ideas that might help:

- Isolating yourself from a hectic life isn't as difficult if you already have everything necessary on hand.
- When looking for an RV, consider one that has at least a ten-foot bed so you can stand up straight while sleeping.
- You should also find an RV with a bathroom and toilet because this is more convenient.
- RVs come in various sizes. A smaller size would be easy to get around and park, but the comfort might be compromised.

Before you start working on making your dream a reality, be sure you have the correct mindset and know what it will take to make it a reality. If you are like most people getting your first RV, it will probably seem complicated and overwhelming at first. But don't let those feelings stop you because you can start by making a few small changes that will help you get comfortable living in the vehicle. Spending time inside your RV will also give you plenty of ideas on how to make it your new home. It is also a good idea to start thinking about the skills and tools you will need for DIY projects in your new RV after determining the initial costs of the RV.

Before moving into your new RV, the first decision you must make is whether it will be mobile or stationary. You should also make sure you can afford the RV's initial fees and that it will fit in the places where you plan to park it.

Building your RV is just a phase of your life, and there are ways in which you can get started on doing it.

Do not forget to plan for necessary items, such as a clothesline or clothes rack, portable grill, camp stove, cooking utensils, towels, and blankets, as well as other essential things such as bedding and so much more.

You need to ensure that you have safe and clean water sources so that you do not have to use bottles or drinking water from any stores.

Planning a route will determine how much time will be spent traveling. A short trip can be made in a day, while a long one would take up to two days.

If you do not have a large trailer, you might want to consider renting one as it can be pricey; but if it is just you and your family, then renting may not be the best option for everyone.

Many people believe that trailers are expensive to buy; however, if you take advantage of the many different discounts and deals out there, then they can actually be very affordable.

A used RV will cost you less money for the initial purchase, while a brand new one will have higher costs, but it also comes with a warranty that can last up to five years.

You should either plan in advance or hire carpenters, plumbers, and electricians to do these things for you, as it is an easier way of getting them done right.

Having a smaller trailer is the best option because there will not be much space to work with, so by keeping it small, you can add more compartments as you go along

When building your own RV, you need to consider all safety features and address all health and safety issues that may arise.

Embracing Minimalism

How People Have Too Much Useless Stuff

Living in an RV can be a transformative experience, but it doesn't always come easy. To make the transition to this more flexible, nomadic lifestyle smoother for you and your family, you'll need to understand what's involved with downsizing your possessions.

That doesn't mean making an unnecessarily massive sacrifice of every object that has any degree of meaning to you; instead, it's about identifying what is necessary as opposed to what is optional or frivolous. There will be an adjustment period, and it may not feel comfortable, but you should not go into this process expecting to lose everything and have to start over.

Instead, downsizing is about moving forward to a new life filled with possibilities. Allow yourself to let go of the past, embrace the future, and get rid of all of your useless material goods.

The good news is that downsizing does not have to be a painful or stressful experience. This book aims to teach you the foundations you'll need to get started.

Thinking about Downsizing?

The road to living in an RV can be long, filled with many decisions and changes. It's tempting to get caught up in the anticipation of all the things you'll do, see, and meet. Moreover, it's equally important not to lose sight of the decision's true significance and how it will profoundly affect your life.

That's why you must take some time and consider all the angles before making an impulsive decision. Decide whether your current lifestyle is actually working for you and decide if you're ready to make a change.

If downsizing your possessions is a natural part of the process of making the transition to an RV life, then proceed to decide how much of your stuff you need. That doesn't necessarily mean that everything that you own has to be sold; it just means identifying what is absolutely essential, which helps you focus your energy on what's actually important.

But if downsizing is something you're undertaking because you feel the pressures of life and are looking to simplify, you have to reevaluate which possessions will make a difference in your life.

If you decide against selling or donating anything, you must realize that new things can be purchased by building up instead of going backward.

Downsizing can also be about planning for a better future and having some fun while getting rid of what's old. New social changes and trends may spur the decision, or it could be a conscious effort to do something "different" for your family. It is necessary to note that there are many things you might take into account when downsizing your possessions, but there are also some that you just shouldn't bother with.

Before moving ahead, venture out and figure out what you need to do before moving on to the next step. Take a look at ten questions that you should ask yourself before getting started.

Purge Your Possessions?

As you consider the answer to the question of whether or not you have too much stuff, it's obvious that it won't be easy to determine that there will ever be a specific number. It is determined by a variety of factors, including how frequently you move, whether or not you have a family, and how much space is available in your current living space.

If you include all your stuff in this conversation, then there's always going to be an overwhelming amount of material possessions, and they aren't necessarily contingent on lifestyle choices.

But if you're looking to simplify your life, then downsizing is a great way to achieve that goal. The whole point of this move is to have less and live more, but you can still follow some basic guidelines as you begin this process. There is no right or wrong answer; it's just about knowing what's right for you.

How much stuff do I own? The first step in this process should be finding out how much stuff you have-literally- that involves tackling every square inch of your living area and all the little spaces where it feels like there's no additional space.

Don't be intimidated by the task of counting everything because it will give you a solid idea of where you stand on the scale. There will always be a minuscule amount of stuff spread across your living area, and if you take this time to get an accurate count, it will put everything into perspective for you.

What's here now? Don't forget to consider what's in your current vehicle and whether or not it's worth keeping once you have downsized to an RV. If an item is in its original package, then there is no point in getting rid of it.

But if it's worn, there's no reason to keep it. The idea is not to get rid of everything you have but to decide what is essential and what you can do without. Don't be discouraged by this process; if the weights listed include the weight of the packaging materials, then you're ahead of many other people because their items may have been included.

Downsizing doesn't have to be a painful process; in fact, it can involve a lot of fun—just like any transition or change in your life! There are many ways that you can save money and still obtain the quality things that you need.

My Approach to Getting Rid of Stuff

You might have a lot of possessions with you right now. Just look around, and you'll find a visual confirmation of that statement.

When you are about to make the shift to living full-time in an RV, you are going to have to make some important decisions. Mostly, you are going to make the not-so-easy choice of figuring out just what you would like to have in your RV. If you quickly assess all the things you have in your home; you are likely going to feel that there are many things that are important to you. But importance does not mean you can take them with you—you can't fit your entire shoe wardrobe into your RV.

You may be thinking about how difficult it will be to part with some of your possessions at this point. You might even wonder if there are others out there who are about to go through the same dilemma you are going to face. Isn't the world heading towards the ownership of more materialistic things rather than walking away from them?

Do you want to know the reality of the situation? People are actually giving up on materialistic possessions in exchange for experiences. In fact, it has been estimated that over 78% of millennials—who have an astonishing $1.3 trillion purchasing power—are choosing to spend that hard-earned money on experiences rather than objects (Power, 2018).

The point is that more and more people are less afraid to give up on things in exchange for something more valuable: the chance to live through something intangible and wonderful. However, the problem they face is not knowing how to keep on living the life they choose. They find themselves saving up some money, traveling to a country and experiencing new things, then returning to their day jobs. Rinse and repeat. They are not able to keep the traveling lifestyle sustainable.

Nevertheless, we are going to not merely travel someplace and return to our daily grind. We are going to keep on traveling for as long as our hearts' desire.

With that idea in mind, it becomes less difficult to get rid of some of the things currently taking up space in your home.

Downsizing for the Count

Let's get down to the nitty-gritty details of the downsizing process. Remember that it makes no difference whether you live in a beachfront mansion or a small studio apartment. Downsizing is a tough job unless you have been living a minimalist lifestyle, in which case, you might find the task of preparing your RV considerably easier.

To clearly explain the concept of downsizing, I have broken down the process into simple steps.

A Downsizing Plan

Your plan brings together various factors to help keep the downsizing process running smoothly. To develop an effective downsizing plan, think of the below points or questions while keeping in mind the space in the RV you are moving into:

- What items from your home can you get rid of?
- What can you absolutely not get rid of?
- How can you donate, sell, or throw away items that you won't need?
- Which items will you donate, sell, or throw away?

Items You Cannot Get Rid of

This is a difficult stage in the downsizing process, primarily because if we ask ourselves what we want to get rid of, we may simply say, "Absolutely nothing!"

But in order to find out what you should keep, think of the following points or questions:

- Are there any items that have sentimental value to you?
- Think of those items that you have spent a lot of money on and loathe to part with it.
- Write a list of the items you have held onto for a long time.
- Do you have objects or items you haven't used yet, but think they hold potential for the future?

Once you have made a list of the items you cannot get rid of, try giving a reason as to why you cannot let go of them.

This is an important step because, oftentimes, we are unsure of the actual reason why we would like to hold on to some things. That pocket watch your father gave you when you were young is something you should always hold on to. But the $300 shoes you bought, thinking they would impress your friends, won't really matter for your RV life. When you start evaluating your arsenal of items with logic and rational thought, then you can actually begin to understand what you should include in your RV and what you can get rid of.

Downsize Your Clothes

Now that you have a pile of clothes you cannot get rid of, look through those items again and pick the pieces you will need while you are RVing. In order to make it a little bit easier on you, here is a list of necessary items:

- Casual t-shirts and shorts
- A few button-up shirts
- A couple of formal wear (or dress) options
- Jeans
- Slacks and track shirts/pants (if you have them)
- Windbreaker and fleece jacket
- Raincoat
- A pair of casual shoes and a pair of formal shoes/shoes that go with formal wear (essentially, nothing that looks appropriate for jogging)
- Hiking boots or boots for cold weather
- Bathrobe
- Night clothes
- Slippers
- Sandals
- Bathroom slippers
- Sunglasses
- Wraparound glasses with wind protection
- A few face masks (for those who have certain allergies or for any other reason that might come up)
- Umbrellas (one should be enough, but you could keep a couple if you have space)

Donate or Sell Your Clothes

While you are downsizing your wardrobe, think about the items that you could donate to a local charity or other non-profit organizations. At this point, you might feel like you have many clothes you would not like to part with, but the key is to think of downsizing in a logical manner. For example, if you have a dozen dresses, pick one or two you really like and keep the rest for donation or sale. It's the same with everything else. If you have a shoe closet with about 200 different pairs of shoes, you won't be needing all of them on your trip. Make a rational decision and let the rest go to someone in need.

Trash Your Clothes

If you have faded clothes, have stains or tears, or might be damaged beyond repair, throw them away. Some people might decide to donate such clothes, but I like to believe that if you don't like wearing them, don't give them to someone else. If you are giving something away, make sure it is in relatively good condition. It's a matter of principle similar to the idea that if you wouldn't eat something, don't give the food to someone else.

Store Some Clothes

You might come across certain clothes that have sentimental value. Don't bring them in your RV. Rather, store them in your home for safekeeping. If there are any other items of clothing you simply must store, then make sure you do it now.

Essential Kitchen Items to Take

You know what they say—if you don't prepare, then you'd better beware.

Actually, nobody said that, but you can't deny that it is true. When you plan ahead, then you are not leaving anything to chance. You're making the right moves and choices to ensure that you have greater control over as many future scenarios as possible. While it is true that the future is unpredictable and that we cannot always plan for every possible outcome, it goes without saying that you should expect the best and prepare for the worst. And yes, somebody actually said that.

Your next course of action is to take all the items you will require in your mobile kitchen. Here is a handy list you can use as a template:

- Dinner plates, coffee mugs, cereal bowls, dessert dishes
- Drinking and wine glasses
- Chef's knife
- Spoons (both tablespoons and teaspoons), forks, and dinner knives
- Whisk
- Grater
- Cutting board
- Can opener
- Measuring cups and measuring spoons
- Colander
- Mixing bowls
- Vegetable peeler
- Potato masher
- Tongs
- Corkscrew or wine bottle opener
- Stainless steel skillet
- Saucepans (one small, one medium, and one large)
- Baking sheet pan
- Casserole dish

- Cookie sheet
- Storage containers
- Aluminum foil
- Plastic wrap
- Oven mittens
- Immersion blender
- Plastic tablecloth
- Table mats, dishcloths, and napkins
- Clips to close bags
- Heavy sponge
- Dishwashing liquid
- Small trash bags
- Coffee pot (get a percolator one on the off chance you don't have a sufficient power source)
- Small grill
- BBQ utensils
- Small toaster

Kitchen Items to Donate or Sell

Here are points to consider when you are donating or selling kitchen items:

- Items that are duplicates.
- You might not need things for an RV, like cheese spreaders, salad spinners, and garlic presses.
- Other items you do not use often.
- Just like your clothing, throw away any kitchen item that is broken, damaged, or rusted.

Essential Bedding/Sofa Items to Take

Time to add a bit of comfort to your RV. For the most part, choosing the items you would like to take for bedding (or sofa, if your RV has one) is fairly simple.

Nevertheless, here is a handy list for inspiration:

- Pillows and a few pillowcases
- At least one change of bed linens
- Comforter
- Blankets
- A few cushions
- Your favorite soft toy, if you have one (hey, no judgment passed—it's your RV!)

Bedding Items to Donate or Sell

- Items that are too bulky or are not required for an RV, such as large cushions, bed linens that are too big, curtains, and anything of the like.
- Any duplicates, ranging from your pillowcases to bedspreads.

Bedding Items to Store

If you have certain items with sentimental value, keep them with you. Plan everything carefully so you don't accidentally give away or sell something that might later prove to be valuable to you or someone else.

Documents to Keep in the RV

There are documents you would like to always have with you, just in case a situation occurs where you might need to show them as proof of something or to complete a process. Below is a list that should help you get started, but feel free to add anything you think is absolutely invaluable.

- Passports, birth certificates, marriage documents, and documents that prove the purchase of the RV.
- Any insurance you may need.
- Multiple passport-size photographs.
- Identification cards, credit cards, insurance cards (if you have them), social security cards (if you have them), and other forms or cards or special identifications.
- If you have important records, such as tax records, consider scanning them and storing them electronically. Since records might be useful, however, you can keep them with you in the RV as well.
- Multiple copies of all the above documents.

Evaluating Future Purchase

If you're considering purchasing an RV, the most crucial factor to consider is how you want to utilize it. You don't want to squander money on something you won't use, so think about what you'll do in your new home before buying anything.

Everyone has a plan in mind when they decide to buy their own RV. Everyone seemed to have a vision of what they will be able to accomplish with their automobile. The most important question is whether these plans will work out and make the investment value in the long run.

First, it's worth considering what type of RV you really want. You can buy an RV bigger than you'll need and which can be very costly. On the other hand, running a smaller vehicle with limited space will cost less fuel and wear and tear on the vehicle. It also saves you money on insurance, registration, and maintenance costs.

Where Things Could Turn Sour

It is true that once you have your home base in an RV, there are many ways to expand your life beyond driving around in your own vehicle. You can hit the road in a few different ways:

You are selling your current residence and completely downsizing to an RV. This will no doubt bring about some savings in expenses, as you won't have so many household payments to worry about anymore. It's also a great way to avoid any sort of mortgage or other loan payments. Once you've sold your home, you'll be able to get rid of a lot of the excess items that you don't need anymore.

Leasing or renting out your home while keeping your RV as an additional place to live; you'll then be able to move around without having to go back and forth from one place to another, as long as you can maintain a steady job.

Enter into a longer-term lease with an RV park. This will allow you to stay in your home while still living in your own camper. You'll be able to spend time at home and maintain a reasonably typical way of life. The downside is that it'll require you to move around as often as is needed for your job, and most likely, you won't live near your job or in a city where there are things to do...

Thirdly, go on the road with friends. You can enjoy great times together without having to worry about paying for all of the expenses of running a house every day.

Another option is to follow a seasonal schedule. This allows you to live the RV lifestyle only during the summer, which is an excellent way to enjoy the outdoors without having to work as hard during the winter.

Lastly, it's important to think about how much time you expect to spend living in your RV and how much time you'll spend on the road. This will help determine how much you need in terms of storage space (it's easier if you have less stuff) or sleeping arrangements.

All of these options can be great fun. The idea of living somewhere different every day can be very exciting when you're starting out with your new life as an RV owner. But there are limits to how far you can go before you have to make a big change.

While some people may be fine with living in an RV their entire lives, others will want something more permanent. It's best to think about your future plans and how much living in an RV will help you achieve your goal.

We hope this advice has been useful, and we wish you the best of luck as you plan your purchase. Once you've made a decision, it's important to move right along rather than take too much time in the planning stage. This will save you money on something that will not work out for you.

Myths to Debunk

There are many misconceptions about living full-time in an RV.

There are some things you need to be concerned about when you're living full-time in an RV (or when you're considering it), but make sure you're concerned about real problems and not untrue ones.

There is a lot of information glorifying the RVing lifestyle and making it sound like it's all sunsets, campfires, and margaritas.

There is also information out there that makes it sound like living the full-time RVing lifestyle is a horrible mistake and something you will regret if you try it.

I want to debunk what I consider to be the eight most prominent untrue myths about the RV lifestyle.

#1. RVs are expensive and a financial disaster. You'll lose your shirt if you buy an RV because they depreciate like mad. This could happen if you buy a new RV and then sell it in a year or two. New RVs depreciate like mad. As your first RV, you should never buy a new one.

When you visit an RV dealership, it's easy to fall in love with one of those new, shiny RVs. On top of that, with payments stretched out over 20 years, new RVs can seem downright affordable.

The problem is that almost all RVers decide they want a different RV after a year or two on the road. I have friends who have had four different types of RVs in the three years they've been on the road. They didn't lose their shirt because they bought each of their RVs at an attractive price. They made a profit in each of the three RVs they have sold.

When you first start living the RV life, you don't know much about RVs, so how could you pick the right one for you?

The second problem is that even if you do a lot of research and become somewhat of an expert on RVs, you will probably still buy the wrong RV because how you want to live will most likely change.

So yes, buying an RV can be expensive, and it can be a financial disaster. That is IF you buy a new RV and then want to sell it in a year or two.

The truth is that if you buy a used (even a very used) RV, do your research and find an RV that's priced below its market value, and you do a good job of negotiating you can buy an RV, keep it a year or two and possibly sell it and make a profit. I know plenty of people who have done this.

Whether buying an RV is expensive and a financial disaster or not depends on how you go about it. For some people, that has proven to be the case. Don't let it happen to you.

#2. Full-time RVing is for retired or rich people only. Not true. A recent industry report said that 40% of the RVs sold last year were sold to young, non-retired people.

A few years ago, it was true that RVers were mostly retired people and a few trust-fund kids, but not anymore. There are many young people and people who are not necessarily young but are not retired or wealthy who live full-time in their RVs.

There are two main reasons why this is happening.

#1. There is a staggering amount of information on the internet (in the form of blogs and YouTube videos) and a lot of books available that tell people about the lifestyle. Other RVers explain how they're doing it, how they're making money (and yes, in many cases, making the lifestyle sound more fun and glamorous than it really is). Just a few years ago, this information was not available. If you didn't know someone personally who was living full time in an RV, information about the lifestyle and how to go about it was hard to come by. That's no longer the case.

#2. The second reason young and non-retired people are hitting the road in RVs is that they can live inexpensively on the road, and it's easy to make more money than it's costing them to live the RVing lifestyle. The internet has suddenly made it easy to make a decent livelihood without doing a traditional job.

Not only can you make money doing work on your computer, but you can use your computer to find what is called "workamping" jobs where you make physical labor (campground hosts, picking fruit and vegetables, working in shops, being a waiter or waitress) and the list of optional ways to make money goes on and on.

You can also sell things on eBay, Amazon, Etsy, etc. I guess that would be a combination of physical work and computer work.

Thinking that you can't afford to live full-time in an RV is no longer a reason not to do it. You can likely live in an RV and put more money into savings than you did when you were working your full-time nine-to-five jobs (I know I do). You probably won't make as much as you're making now, but your living expenses can be reduced considerably by taking advantage of boondocking and other free camping options.

#3. Extremely low gas mileage makes RV travel almost prohibitive. It's true that RVs don't get great gas mileage. I get about eight mpg in my 34-foot, Class A motorhome when I'm towing my car. Smaller RVs get a lot better gas mileage, but let's use my beast of a gas hog as a worst-case example.

I've seen gas priced below $2.00 a gallon in several places lately. At eight mpg and gas priced at $2.00 a gallon, that's 25 cents a mile or $25 to drive 100 miles.

If you travel all the time, want to take a trip to Alaska, or want to visit every national park in one year, you could rack up some miles, but most RVers don't do that. Some travel a lot in the first year, but then they realize that RVing is more enjoyable if they slow down.

I like to stay in one place for at least a month. If I stay in one place for a month and then drive 200 miles to the next place, that would mean that I would be spending $50 a month on gas. Even if I only stayed in one place for one week and then drove 200 miles to my next location, I would be driving 800 miles a month and spending $200 a month on gas. You may be spending more than $200 a month on gas now.

The truth is that what you'll spend on gas as a full-time RVer is almost a non-issue. To make things even better, you can cut your gas expenses down to zero for a month or two anytime you want by just not driving. You don't have to always be driving. You can stay and enjoy the area once you've found somewhere you like. That's what I do. Also, your next location is probably not going to be 200 miles away.

#4. Live the RVing lifestyle, and your problems will go away. A lot of RVing videos, blogs, and books make the RV lifestyle sound like it would make all your problems go away. Not so. It could even add to your problems. RVing won't change who you are.

For instance, if you and your spouse don't get along, you will probably not get along as well as you do now if you start living in an RV. If you're having financial problems, you will continue to have financial problems unless you change the way you spend money.

When you start living the RV lifestyle is a great time to get rid of a lot of baggage (both literally and figuratively). It's a good time to make changes to your life, but don't expect the changes to happen automatically.

#5. RVs are way too small for full-time living. When people start thinking about downsizing from a house to an RV, they usually think they need a big RV.

Most people who have been RVing for a long time realize that their RV is far too large (me included). When buying their second RV, almost everyone I know has gone to a smaller RV.

For example, after five years on the road living in a 17-foot Casita camper, Becky Schade (author of the RV blog, InterstellarOrchard.com) sold her "big" 17-foot camper and bought a 13-foot teardrop type camper. The smaller camper allows her to get to more remote boondocking places.

Of all the things you need to consider and be concerned with, your RV being too small to live in comfortably will not be one of them, at least not after you have lived in your RV for a while.

You probably don't believe me now, but take my word for it and move on to worrying about something else.

#6. Trying to RV with kids is a nightmare. A lot of RVing families disagree with this statement. They love the amount of time they get to spend with their kids and getting to watch them grow up.

You can RV if you have kids—here's how:

Children adapt well to life on the road. They get to see and experience so much more of life and the real world than they would in a classroom or a typical neighborhood. With home-schooling and the internet, traveling with kids (of any age) is a very viable option.

Here are some videos that will let you see for yourself what RVing with kids is like.

- Youtube.com/watch?v=z4QSp28ymvQ – Nate, Marissa, and their young daughter enjoying the RVing lifestyle.
- Youtube.com/watch?v=BsEs-CLBbaU&t-98s – Marc and Tricia travel with their kids and have posted several fun, interesting, and informative RVing videos.
- Youtube.com/watch?v=c2xkfkhfcEg – Nate and Christian Axness are a young couple who travel with their two kids. I think you will find their videos interesting. Here's another one of their videos: Youtube.com/watch?v=xKLparutJhk&t=149s
- On December 4th, 2016, Brittany and Eric brought Caspian (or baby nomad, as they sometimes call him) home from the hospital and moved him into their Class A motorhome when he was one day old. If you want to know more about how this is working out, you can follow them on their blog at RVwanderlust.com/one-year-old-rv

#7. RV repair costs will eat you alive. RV repair costs can get expensive if you have all your repair work done at an RV repair shop.

#8. People who live in RVs are broke and can't afford a house. This is a bonus myth that I wanted to explain. RVers no longer worry about keeping up with the Joneses. It doesn't matter whether you have a $3,000 RV or a $300,000 RV. Surprisingly, some people who live and travel in a $3,000 RV could easily afford a $300,000 RV.

There are a few RVers who live in an RV because they can't afford a house, but most RVers live in an RV by choice and not by necessity. You won't find riff-raff in RV parks or boondocking areas.

Just because many RVers spend a lot of time camping in boondocking areas (national parks, on government-owned BLM land, and in other free camping areas), it's not because they can't afford to pay and camp in an RV park. It's just that they are being frugal. And besides, I've experienced some of the most fun and enjoyable camping when boondocking.

Part II

—

Tips for Buying an RV

Choosing the Right RV for You

Points to Remember Before Buying an RV

Length

"I can't visit national parks if my RV is too long!"

Let me put an end to this rumor right now. While many roads and campgrounds in national parks have vehicle length restrictions, this does not mean you cannot bring your RV there. Take, for example, Grand Teton National Park. The length of Moose Wilson Road is limited to 23 feet. Oh, my goodness! You are not allowed to enter the park.

Wrong. Simply enter through one of the many other unrestricted entrances.

However, RVs under 30 feet are not permitted at Signal Mountain Campground! True. However, Gros Ventre Campground allows RVs up to 45 feet in length. And here's a surprise: in most states, the maximum length for a motorhome is 45 feet. So, you can go to the park even if you buy a 45-foot diesel pusher.

When it comes to length, I completely understand your concern. However, national parks and camping go hand in hand. Even if you have a large rig, you will be able to visit the park. Plus, if you're in an RV that's longer than 30 feet—one of the most common limits we see—you'll almost certainly have a tow car that can take you anywhere. Buses are also available in some parks. In Glacier National Park, we took the public bus up Going-to-the-Sun Road (24-foot limit).

Don't let the fear of missing out on national parks influence your decision-making. Several factors determine your rig's length, but the most important ones are weight and floor plan.

Weight

Weight is important if you plan on purchasing a trailer or camper. You'll need to consider your truck's towing capacity as well as the rig's GVW (gross vehicle weight). Keep in mind that you will add weight to the rig once you move in, so give yourself a large cushion between your towing capacity and vehicle weight.

When it comes to motorhomes, weight is less important. (You will, however, want to look at what weight the motorhome can tow.) Roughly half of all states will require a special driver's license if your RV is over a certain weight. Every state has different requirements, so check yours, but in general, if your RV weighs more than 26,000 pounds, you'll need a special license. This usually means diesel RVs in the 40+ foot range.

Floor Plan

When it comes to picking your perfect length for an RV, weight is vital to consider, but the floor layout is usually the deciding factor. Consider what is absolutely necessary for your setup. Perhaps you are certain that you will require an oven, two bathrooms, or sleeping quarters for eight people.

We knew we required a kitchen layout that had two table tops for working and an oven and plenty of counter space. We only have two people in our family, so a 30–35-foot rig would be ideal.

To get an idea of what length rig you'll need, check out floor plans on manufacturer's websites. YouTube is also a treasure trove of RV walk-through and tour videos so you can get a feel for an RV.

Slide Outs

I mentioned slide-outs before, but I didn't explain what they are. Slide-outs (also known as pop-outs or simply slides) are segments of your RV that slide out when you park to increase living space. (If you're thinking to yourself, "Alyssa, that's the stupidest definition I've ever heard," you're probably correct. BUT, as I drove down the highway, I had to explain slides to a lot of perplexed people who thought my RV was 12 feet wide. No way.)

Slides are the most effective way to expand living space. If you want a smaller rig with plenty of space, this is the way to go. This is ideal if you want a smaller rig with plenty of space.

Slides are most commonly found on class A, C, and super C motorhomes, as well as fifth wheels and travel trailers. Depending on the manufacturer, slides can be electric or hydraulic. In a motorhome, you will still be able to walk around the RV with the slides in. This is typically not possible in fifth wheels and some trailers.

The pièce de résistance is when you have opposing slides. That is, slide-outs directly across from each other. This is what gives you ample floor space. In our Winnebago, I can do yoga in our floor space, and Heath can still walk around me in the rig. Finding a rig with opposing slides is essential if you prefer a more open concept layout.

You should expect to have problems with your slides at some point in your life. They are known to be picky, but the extra space is well worth it. Four times, we've had problems with our slides.

We read a few negative remarks and evaluations concerning full-length slides after we bought our rig (ours spans about 30 feet from the driver's chairs to the bedroom). We've had our large slide worked on three times before; the slide was not coming in correctly in each case. The front would arrive first, followed by the back, or vice versa. This causes the slide to be angled rather than coming in straight. Our slide used to be 6 inches out in the back and not at all in the front because the difference was so large. It had been a nightmarish experience!

According to the mechanic, this is known as being "out of time." He re-timed the motors in the front and back of the slide to operate at the same speeds once more. He claims that this happens frequently, particularly with larger slides carrying a lot of weight. After the third occurrence, the world's sweetest mechanic asked, "Do you want to learn how to prevent this and fix it yourself?"

YES, YES, I DO.

Here's what I learned: To re-time slides that are coming in at different speeds, push out your slide. When you notice that one side is going faster than the other, stop and start bringing the slide back in. Bring the slide in until it looks like the slide is in a straight line again. If you have wood planks or tiles on your floor, the easiest way to measure this is if the slide is parallel to the lines on the floor. Then start pushing it back out again. Keep doing this back and forth, watching the floor to make sure you keep the slide from going out at an angle. This will help the slide correct itself before it gets too out of time.

We did this back and forth finagling every time we noticed our slides getting slightly out of time and never visited the mechanic with slide issues again.

Height

Here's how it works with height: It's not a big deal. Low clearances are uncommon, particularly in the west and south, and they are marked with multiple warning signs and, in some cases, signs for alternate routes if the clearance is low enough. Low clearances are unlikely to prevent you from visiting a specific location, but they may alter your route.

We never have to worry about low clearances with All Stays, Co-Pilot, and our Rand McNally GPS. At least one of these should be used to check for clearances along your route. Our Rand McNally GPS is embedded into our RV, and we've programmed our preferences into it, so we know it won't take us down risky roads.

In all our years of full-timing, we've only found ourselves in one terrible must-U-turn-now situation with low clearances—knock on wood.

We were driving on I-95 from Connecticut to New York City when Heath took the wrong exit, one with about fifty bright orange signs. WARNING: 8 FOOT CLEARANCE AHEAD signs. (He claimed he didn't see any of them.)

We were flagged down by a nice guy in a pickup truck who told us that we should follow him back to the interstate if we wanted to keep our roof. We were back on track in no time, and I'm now a backseat driving queen to ensure we never find ourselves in another heart-stopping situation like this again!

Types of RVs

Motorhomes

Motorhomes are RVs that you can drive and come in various sizes, from basic to luxury models. Depending upon the make, their features and sizes are further categorized into the following types of motorhomes.

Class A Motorhome

Class A motorhomes are designed around the chassis of trucks, a specially designed motor vehicle, or a commercial luxury bus. Most of the time, the front of this motorhome resembles a bus in design, with the front being flat and vertical and the sidewalls having large windows. Its popular slide-outs allow it to have a bigger area as compared to other RVs.

Class B Motorhome

The design imitates that of a van, which has a raised roof. Naturally, it has a smaller area and is not wide like a class A motorhome.

Class C Motorhome

The design is along the lines of a truck chassis and attached to the cab part of the truck. These are deemed as perfect RVs for all kinds of people. Class C motorhomes will fulfill your camping requirements, whether you're singles, a couple, or a family.

Truck Camper

These are known to be the most versatile type of RVs available in the market. Truck Campers are capable of going anywhere, just like a regular pickup truck. In fact, they hook right at the back of a truck above the truck bed.

Pop-up Camper or Fold Downs

It's the best for the new family that is just entering the marketplace of towable RVs. Families have used these for camping over the years. Most of the time, Pop-ups are the first choice of new RVers. Given their lightweight, they are towable by even the smallest of vehicles.

Travel Trailer

These are probably the most common type of RVs you will get to see on campgrounds and roads around you. There are many floor plans to choose from to suit the demands of any RVer. It is easily towed using a frame or a bumper hitch.

Expandable Trailer

Expandable RVs can be towed by medium-sized vehicles using a frame or a bumper hitch. These are treated to be similar to the pop-up camper except that they have hard material sides, in contrast to the tent material that comes with the pop-up camper. Consumers often treat these as an upgrade to pop-up campers, given the sidewalls that are very durable. Many expendables come with a living space, kitchen space and bathroom, and also slide-outs.

Fifth-wheel Trailer

These are the largest type of towable RVs. Large pickup trucks are used to tow these using a fifth-wheel hitch. They come with large living spaces and can be easily towed because of their size.

Toy Hauler

Toy Haulers are actually considered to be a sub-category of class C motorhomes. The name comes from the fact that it has enough area to actually accommodate your toys, such as snowmobiles, motorbikes, ATVs, and even certain four-wheelers.

How To Buy An RV?

Buying an RV is not rocket science. You don't need the help of a car mechanic or engineer to inspect and buy an RV. Before you complete your purchase, there are a few things you should double-check on your own.

RV is not normal household stuff that you buy on a regular basis. It is better to go step by step when purchasing an RV rather than do it in a rush and regret it after some time.

Select Your RV

The moment you decide to move into an RV, you should first decide upon the type of RV. Ask yourself the following questions, and it will help you make the right choice.

- Do you want to buy a brand new RV or a second-hand vehicle?
- Are you planning to move in full time, or do you want an RV just for short trips?
- In what type of locality will you mostly move around? Is it going to be a highway? Or busy roads of downtown?
- Do you need an additional bathroom facility?
- What size of RV can you drive comfortably?

Thoroughly analyze the features, pros, and cons of the types of RVs mentioned above and then have your pick. This is the first and most important step in buying an RV, especially if you intend to live in it full-time. Your choice will have a significant impact on your RV lifestyle.

Find a Dealer

Once you made up your mind on which type of RV you want, the next step is to look for RV dealers. Search online, look in eBay motors, newspaper classifieds, and auctions. Also, meet some of the local RV dealers, tell them your preferences and take advice from them on which type of RV is best for you and where you will find it.

Negotiate the Price

Now that you know what specifications you want in your RV research a bit on the current market price of your selected RV. The best time to buy a second-hand RV is at the end of summer, as many families sell their RVs after coming back from vacations. Never agree on the first price. RV dealers are known for high markups. Negotiate as much as you can. Search online for the market price of the RV that you plan to buy. You must have a price in mind before you negotiate with the dealer.

Checklist for Inspection

Inspect the RV for the following things before you finalize the purchase. Take a printout of the following checklist with you when you go for a test drive or inspect the RV, especially if you are buying a second-hand RV.

Interior Inspection

- Look for any cracks in the flooring.
- Water leakage.
- Exhaust and overhead vent fans.
- Do the overhead vent fans work?
- Run the air conditioner for a few minutes.
- Windows and doors - Do they open and close smoothly?
- Toilet flushes.
- Kitchen accessories.
- Connections for electronic equipment.
- Storage space.
- Any rodents or pest presence.
- Holding tank levels.
- Water pump switch.
- Safety equipment, such as fire extinguisher, smoke detector, security alarm, and emergency exit.
- Brake controls, horn, navigation system, windshield wipers.
- Check the level of battery electrolyte. A low level indicates that the battery has not been properly taken care of.

Exterior Inspection

- Condition of the tires.
- Dents or damage to the external body.
- How stable and balanced is the rear ladder.
- Any signs of rust.
- Check the roof for dents or cracks.
- External lighting and headlamps.
- Slide in and slide out compartments.
- Engine coolant and wiring.

Collect the Documents

Once you are done with the inspections and about to finalize the deal, make sure you obtain the following documents from the RV owner.

- RV manuals.
- Engine manuals.
- Repair and maintenance records.
- Warranty documentation for all major components, battery, and appliances.

Why You Should Never Buy a Brand-New RV

Buying a brand new RV is not as simple as it sounds. The RV industry has grown in popularity and profit, so factory production capacity has been increased without regard to quality control or safety.

The lower-quality manufacturers are taking advantage of this to produce vehicles for sale at bargain-basement prices, but they have learned to make these vehicles cheaply and quickly by sacrificing quality control.

They have also been able to increase production due to the lack of quality control and because they are finding ways to perform all the necessary maintenance on RVs while driving around in them. This means that every model manufactured has 2 or 3 critical problems from which people will die.

RVs have become increasingly like fashion items, being rapidly changed by each model year because of the expectation that they will continue to be produced for another year. However, some models fail in their production stage and are never fixed (commonly referred to as "trim" problems). These rarely occur, but it is a very common occurrence in many lesser-quality manufacturers.

Many people believe that they can buy these vehicles "as is" because of the warranty included in their purchase price. They have been sold a bill of goods due to the lack of quality control and disregard for safety.

To make matters worse, many dealers are not willing to find out about critical problems before selling an RV, so they make it appear that everything is fine when it isn't. They will even tell you that the problems are minor so they can move you along and get your money. Most dealers are in business to sell RVs sold by their local RV dealer.

These dealers sometimes deliberately give bad information to unsuspecting customers in order to milk them for more money. Some dealers may even be promoting unsafe or questionable practices on their websites.

Many people who purchase an RV from a dealer find that they have a problem within the first year after purchase, often when the dealer is not available to help them obtain help. This lack of roadside assistance can turn lives upside down, including losing everything and being forced to remain in an unsafe vehicle.

Manufacturers are not legally required to accept any return of a vehicle that has been driven, even if it is defective. This leaves the consumer with nowhere to turn. In many cases, both the manufacturer and the dealer will ignore the consumer because they know that the person will not have proof of purchase, and there is nothing they can do about it.

Some consumers have abandoned their vehicles. They were able to abandon the vehicle at no cost because their credit card company would allow them an extended warranty, which gave them an excuse for abandoning the unit at no charge.

Before purchasing a new RV from any dealer, you should be aware of all these things and how they could apply to you before making your purchase.

If you do not have a problem, then, by all means, buy an RV. I am just trying to save you from issues that are common among RVs that are sold at the cheaper end of the market. Please get this information out so people will be aware of these problems before they purchase.

Another reason that you should never buy a brand new RV is that their initial build quality is often way below what any other vehicle made by the same manufacturer would be in that same class or price range. The design and engineering processes may also be below par.

A brand new RV that is manufactured by a company that builds quality products will sacrifice some of the design and engineering features to be able to deliver a higher quality RV in the long run.

For example, look at two Class A diesel pushers: an upgraded Alpine Coach vs. a poorly made Thor ACE. Both would be considered entry-level luxury motorhomes, costing about $340,000. The Alpine has more features and nicer finishes than the Thor, but it also weighs over 17,800 lbs. The Thor weighs in at 13,000 lbs., which is over 4,600 less than the Alpine and almost 2 tons lighter than some other diesel pushers of similar size.

The Alpine weighs 173% more than the Thor, over 5,000 lbs. It is designed and engineered to be better at being lighter weight and delivering a higher quality level with less weight.

Another example would be two high-end Class A diesel pushers: a Solaris vs. a Holiday Rambler Vesta. The Solaris costs $340,000, which is considerably more than the Holiday Rambler Vista that is being sold for $160,000. The Solaris has more features and nicer finishes than the Holiday Rambler Vista, but it also weighs over 20,000 lbs. The Holiday Rambler Vista weighs in at 8,300 lbs. It is designed and engineered to be heavier than the Solaris and deliver a lower quality level with more weight.

The Holiday Rambler Vista weighs 229% more than the Solaris, almost 10,000 lbs. It is designed and engineered to be better at being heavier weight and to deliver a lower level of quality with more weight.

Examine these two Class A diesel pushers some more: an upgraded Alpine Coach vs. another Alpine Coach from about 2008 that has been updated on the latest updates for improved performance and safety. The two units come with the same number of features and finishes. The initial cost for both is about $340,000. Both were built by the same company (Alpine Coach). And yet, one unit weighs 17,800 lbs., whereas the other weighs 8,700 lbs.

The 17,800 lb. Alpine has more features and better finishes than the 8,700 lb. Alpine. But it also has almost 10,000 lbs. of excess weight to carry around every day. That is because each one has a different design and engineering approach to its construction as well as different components that have been selected for use in each unit based on their design tradeoffs that were made during the design process between the years 2007 and 2017 (when Alpine ceased manufacturing).

The 8,700 lb. Alpine does not have as many features or finishes to compare with. But it still has almost 3,000 lbs. of excess weight to carry around every day. That is because each one has a different design and engineering approach to its construction as well as different components that have been selected for use in each unit based on their design tradeoffs that were made during the design process between the years 2008 and 2017 (when Alpine ceased manufacturing).

These two units both share the same manufacturing plant and QC departments. The only difference is that one unit weighs 17,800 lbs. whereas the other weighs 8,700 lbs. The 8,700 lb. Alpine is superior to the 17,800 lb. Alpine in this case.

If you look at a line of RVs that are considered entry-level luxury Class A diesel pushers, such as Thor ACE vs. the larger Thor Octane that was introduced in 2014, you will see these same differences. The Octane is much heavier than the ACE, but it also has superior quality. And yet, people still buy the cheaper ACE instead of paying extra for a unit with an upgraded design and increased engineering and components that are not used in the lesser models. Both units have similar features and finishes in many cases, yet, one weighs nearly 2 tons more than the other.

If you want to compete with the Alpinas and Thors, then you should be willing to do the same in your own manufacturing facilities. But not if you want to sell RVs at a lower price.

Another reason why people buy brand-new RVs is that they are often overpriced due to all of these reasons and many more. And yet, people still do it because of one reason: it is the style.

Some people want all the best and latest features at a high price point without worrying about weight, quality, reliability, or resale value. They are buying an RV that is built with a high level of quality and engineered to last.

It is just a big fashion statement to many of these people. They do not buy it for quality or reliability; they buy it for style and the status it provides them. If the unit delivers on all of its promises, then great! But if it does not, then you are stuck with something that you have no control over the future of after you buy it.

An RV buyer should look at his or her options before buying an entry-level luxury RV and evaluate the tradeoffs between the quality, reliability, and resale values of each different RV in a given class. But for many people, style is more important than these other factors.

I think that most customers looking for an entry-level luxury RV are looking at their options and choosing based on their choice of features, finishes, and engineering design process over a long period of time. But some people just buy it because it is just what they want. It makes them feel good about themselves when they pick out all the expensive features that are advertised in a brochure on TV. They just want to feel like a big shot when sticking out their leg to show off the table with a leather skirt and fancy footstool. It is just easier for many people to buy an entry-level luxury RV than it is for them to think about what they are actually getting into.

Another reason people buy an entry-level luxury RV is that they just do not know any better. They do not realize that those shiny things in the brochure are fake and have no value. They tend to be in the higher price categories for most of these brands (even if a company advertises prices lower than those shown in the brochure). And there are different levels of options within each brand that make up these costs. Some people buy an entry-level luxury RV to save money but then are not prepared to deal with the hassle and maintenance problems that all these luxury units have. Others get out of their vehicle after work and make the drive in a few hours at a time. If they buy an expensive low-quality RV without thinking it through, then they will get into trouble sooner than most people.

Part III

–

RV Driving & Testing

How to Learn to Drive Your RV

In a Nutshell, Here's How to Drive an RV

One approach to learning how to drive an RV is to just get in and start driving and hope that you and the RV both survive until you learn how to drive it. I think a lot of people use this approach, but there's a better way.

This is not intended to make you an expert RV driver just by reading it, but my intentions are to cover enough driving instructions to convince you that you can become a great RV driver.

When you first start driving your RV, it will feel like you're driving a battleship. You will feel like you're taking up all of your lane and half of the opposing lane.

While you're driving, glance at the four or six mirrors (two or three on each side) and make sure that you can see the painted line on the highway on both sides of your lane. This will reassure you that you are exactly where you need to be, even if it doesn't feel like it. After a little while driving, it will become second nature, and your subconscious mind will take over, and driving down the road will finally feel normal.

Keep in mind that everyone has a tendency to crowd the right side of the road. This is OK when you're meeting a big truck on a two-lane road, but for normal driving, just keep it equally between the center line and the edge of the road line. The person in the co-pilot seat will feel like you are way too far to the right, and the co-pilot will feel like you're going way too fast. To me, when I'm in the right seat, it looks like I'm about to straddle the white line on the edge of the road—but when I look in the side mirror, I see that the rig is right inside the edge of the road line where it should be.

How to Turn to the Right

The front wheels on most Class A rigs turn 50 degrees, so a good rule of thumb to remember when making right-hand turns is to pull forward far enough so that your hips are just past the curb, signpost, or whatever it is you want to miss. Then turn as sharp as you can to the right. Of course, glance at the signpost or curb that you want to miss while making the turn.

Also, on right-hand turns, watch the back, left corner of your rig. The back part that's behind the rear tires will swing out to the left. Watch and make sure your back end doesn't swing over and hit a car in the lane beside you. And if you're pulling out of camping space, make sure your back end doesn't swing out and hit the RV beside you.

When making a turn at an intersection, if you find that you can't make the turn without crossing into the oncoming lane, simply stop and wait for the traffic to clear, then cross over into the lane and continue on your way. You probably won't receive the RV driver of the year award (at least, not from the people having to wait behind you), but you will never see them again anyway, so it doesn't matter. Don't try to back up and never back up if you're pulling a toad.

How to Turn to the Left

When you're turning left, you have a lot more room, and you can make a wide turn with no problem. Be sure to pull forward and make a reasonably sharp turn. Don't make a haphazard turn and let the back left corner of your RV go over and hit the car waiting at the intersection for you to make your turn.

Walmart Can Help You Learn to Drive

The best way to learn to drive your RV is to spend an hour or so in a Walmart parking lot early on a Sunday morning when it's almost empty. Get off in a corner by yourself. Set up some empty cardboard boxes and practice making turns. Notice how the back end swings out wider than the back wheels when you make a sharp turn. It's easy to forget about the back end swinging around.

When you're in the Walmart parking lot, line your RV up so that the edge of the coach is even with one of the painted stripes that mark a parking space. Have your co-pilot stand outside as you make a sharp turn. Have them mark how wide the back of your RV swings past the parking spaceline. This is your over-swing.

Knowing this distance can prevent you from causing costly damage to your RV and other vehicles. When you do this exercise and actually see what happens, it makes the concept of over-swing more real than just reading about it.

How much space do you need to make a turn? Have someone stand six feet in front of your RV. Then slowly make a sharp turn. You should just miss them. Have them note how much you missed them or how far they had to back up to avoid being hit.

Knowing all of these measurements will make you a good and safe driver. Most RV drivers don't actually know this information about their rigs. They just wing it.

Backing Your RV

Other people tell me that they think they could drive an RV, but they're not sure about being able to back it into those camping spaces. You can back into tight spaces blindfolded—you really can, because all you have to do is listen to the person directing you. You turn right when you are told to (or signaled to turn), and you turn left when you are told to.

One other important thing is that you also stop when you are told to. Backing an RV is a lot easier than backing a trailer. Turning the steering wheel to the right causes the back of the RV to move to the right and vice versa. What could be easier? Of course, you have to turn the steering wheel in the opposite direction you want the back end to go when backing a fifth-wheel or trailer.

I have six mirrors and a backup camera to see what's going on behind me, but I trust the person standing behind the rig more.

In other words, don't worry about backing. You can do it like a pro. Just watch for the hand signals in your mirrors and listen to what your lookout person is telling you. The backup camera has a microphone, and the sound comes in loud and clear through the rearview monitor system.

And as an extra precaution, the rearview camera has a grid superimposed on the color screen showing you what's 3 ft., 2 ft., 1 ft., and then zero feet behind you.

While you're in the Walmart parking lot, take the time to practice backing. Use your cardboard boxes and assume that they are other RVs or power poles. Most of the time, when you're backing, you will have someone guiding you. An important point is that if you can't see the person who is guiding you, STOP. Don't keep backing and assume that everything is all right. Try backing with someone helping you, and then while you're at it, try backing all by yourself, just using your backup camera and mirrors.

If you don't have a co-pilot, there are always other RVers available to help you, but proceed with caution. I was at a campground one time, and a guy was backing into a camping spot. A woman was guiding him, and the top corner of his RV rubbed against a big tree limb. Luckily, there was no major damage. The woman said, "I wasn't watching that side." Duh?

The backup camera is your plan B to make sure you don't back into a post or big rock. With a little experience, you should be able to back into a spot by yourself by using the mirrors and the backup camera, but I always like to have someone back there saying, "'mon-back" and then "stop" as my plan A.

More Points about Driving

Go over speed bumps very slowly, and if at all possible, go over them straight on so that both front tires hit them at the same time. If you go over them at an angle, you're going to get four bumps instead of two, and the resulting twisting of your RV could cause glasses in the cabinet to tumble out into the floor and maybe even cause seams in the roof to crack. This could cause leaks. Measure your RV's height from the ground to the highest point (usually the top of the air conditioners). You will be OK going under Interstate highway overpasses, but be careful on back-road overpasses, tunnels, and especially at service stations.

Nothing beats the experience of just driving down the Interstate to get the feel of driving your RV. The more you drive it, the more comfortable you will feel doing it, and who knows, one day, you might just receive the RV driver of the year award (if there is such a thing).

An RV Driving Course Manual

There's a good RV driving course manual available for $30 at RvBasicTraining.com. I own this book, and I highly recommend it. If you're going to spend $30,000 to buy an RV, spend another $30 and learn how to drive it.

This is a 46-page manual, but there are a lot of pictures and drawings included in the 46 pages, so it's not that much actual reading. If you read this manual and do a few of the parking lot exercises, you will know more about how to drive an RV than most of the drivers on the road.

Sign Up for an RV Driving Course

Of course, the ideal thing to do is to sign up for an RV driving class. Search Google for the phrase "RV driving class" or "RV driving school," and you will find when and where there is a class being held in your area.

The classes usually run a full day, with part of the time in a classroom and part of the time with you actually driving your RV. The costs typically run about $300 to $500 for the day.

As one friend of mine put it when you're in a class A RV, you're sitting up high, and even if someone hits you broadside, you probably wouldn't be hurt, and your rig is covered by insurance, so don't worry. Just go enjoy the journey. I don't know if I like his way of thinking, but I guess it's true.

Licensing

In most cases, driving a motorhome does not necessitate a special license. Generally, no special license is required if your RV is less than 40 feet long and weighs less than 26,000 pounds.

Plan Ahead

One last point. To be a good RV driver, you need to think and plan ahead. Don't pull into places you can't get out of. Remember, you can't back an RV if you're pulling a toad. When pulling into or out of a service station, restaurant, etc., go slow, watch all corners of your RV and, by all means, watch out for your overhead clearance. If it even looks closely, stops and get out and look or have someone get out and look.

How to Test Your RV

Now that you have made a choice, you need to test the RV to make sure it is road-worthy. It would be devastating to get a few miles down the road and discover the brakes are in bad shape or the motorhome shifts hard. This is a list of the items you will want to check for to make sure your RV is in sound condition.

Exterior

1. Headlights
2. Tail lights
3. Blinkers, hazard lights
4. Backing lights
5. Clearance lights
6. Awning rollout
7. Slides work without getting stuck
8. Steps are easy to slide out and in good condition
9. No signs of leaks—rust or discoloration on the outside walls
10. Seals around windows are intact
11. The roof is in good condition
12. Check storage compartments for signs of leakage
13. Check fuel doors and caps
14. Inspect generator
15. Inspect holding tanks

Interior

1. Heater, defrosters
2. Automatic seats
3. Window controls
4. Automatic locks
5. Air conditioner—throughout RV
6. Fans
7. Automatic mirrors
8. Kitchen appliances all work
9. Fans work
10. Cabinets are in good condition with latching mechanisms functional
11. Floor/carpeting in good, clean condition
12. Press up on the ceiling to detect sagging, which indicates leaking

13. Pull out foldout beds to make sure they are in good condition
14. Check caulking around the sink, and under the cabinet to look for signs of leaking
15. Flush the toilet, run the shower and sink to test
16. Ensure any televisions and other entertainment systems work
17. Check to make sure windows open easily, and screens are in place

Road Test

1. East start, no difficulties
2. The engine idle should be smooth
3. Acceleration is smooth—doesn't cut out
4. Transmission shifts easily
5. Braking responds appropriately with service and exhaust
6. Cruise control works
7. Steering is responsive, not loose
8. Temperature gauges work
9. Tracking is smooth
10. Cornering is smooth and responsive
11. Engine noise level is appropriate, not overly loud
12. No odd sounds, i.e., pings, groans, or squealing noises
13. Four-wheel drive mode works if equipped

Make sure you take the RV on the highway. You need to get a feel for how it rides, as well as the power of the engine. A weak engine is likely not in good condition and would need a tune-up. A tune-up may uncover more serious problems.

Some cosmetic issues are fixable. It is important to determine the cost of repairs and if it is worth investing in. Spend some time going over every inch of the RV before you make an offer. Open every cabinet, turn on every light, drive the RV in town and on the highway, and do your best to put it through the paces to identify any potential issues.

Take somebody with you who is familiar with RVs and will know what to look for. Consider printing a checklist of the internet to help you remember every detail. Never take the seller's word that something works. Test it for yourself!

Part IV

—

Pros, Cons, and Essential Tips

How Much Does RV Living Cost?

I wish we could just give you a number! But there are numerous, almost countless, factors that will impact your full-time RVing budget. What we'll do in this is list those factors, try to give you an approximation, and get you started on your full-time RV budget.

And believe me, for an RVer, making a budget can save your financial life.

Once you've got your RV, full-time RV living can be surprisingly affordable—or surprisingly expensive—like any other kind of living. Planning is the key; know as much as you can to go as far as you can.

The Financial Questions You'll Need to Ask Are

What Are My Campsite Costs?

This will depend on whether you'll be staying in RV parks, state parks, or boondocking (off the grid). RV parks and campgrounds can cost the most money. Where you stay offers the most financial flexibility. Like anywhere else, the more luxurious your lifestyle, the higher your 'rent.' One relatively new option is RV Host websites which offer you the opportunity to find places to stay hosted by fellow RVers.

RV Parks

RV parks with full hookups (water, electricity, sewer) will cost between $30–$60 per night. The most convenient, especially since you can shower, fill up your potable water, and dump your waste tanks without spending additional money. Your monthly expense: between $900–$1600.

State Park Campgrounds

State (and in some places, County) park campgrounds can be quite beautiful and are often quieter than RV parks. The fees vary by location and amenities. Look them up in advance because the fees are low, and many require advance reservations. You'll also want to find out what, if any, hookups they offer. Campgrounds with water and electricity cost from $20–$30 per night. Many State park campgrounds without hookups can be found for around $15–$20 per night. Caveat:

Don't plan on making a State park your home for too long. Most of them have a limit on how many consecutive nights you can stay. Monthly expense: with hookups—$600; without hookups—$360.

Boondocking

Boondocking is camping without hookups. There are Federal Bureau of Land Management locations and State forests around the country that have free camping areas. Most of these places limit your stay to 14 consecutive days. Here again, the Internet can be a great resource for finding boondocking spots that are really off the grid. Remember that, although the sites are free, it will be up to you to find and pay for dump stations and potable water.

RV Hosting Websites

If you search for "RV Hosting," you'll find a growing number of membership websites that allow you to camp at members' locations for an annual fee, many of which are free. Boondockers Welcome costs $25 per year and gives you the opportunity to stay on property owned by member hosts across the country for no additional charge. Harvest Hosts specializes in wineries and farms that offer boondocking space. Every week, it appears that there are more of these websites. At $25–$45 per year, these sites pay for themselves quickly.

What Will I Need to Spend on Gas, Insurance, Repairs, and Maintenance?

Gas expenses are, of course, difficult to calculate. Prices change by region and by day. One way to estimate is this: figure your average gas mileage. If you're towing, calculate the mileage while towing. Map out your trip on Google Maps and determine how many miles you'll be traveling. If you know your stops well in advance, put them all in there! Find the average gas prices for the areas in which you'll be traveling. If you go coast to coast, use the national average (also available online). That's as close as you can get.

RV Insurance is also not an easy calculation because of the factors it's based upon. Price of the RV, your age, gender, marital status, credit score, how many miles you drive, and how many days a year you'll be using it (usually grouped into plus or minus 150 days). For a full-time RVer, it's a combination of vehicle insurance and homeowner's insurance. And choose a provider that offers full RV coverage, not just an add-on to car insurance.

When you live in an RV full time, one rule to remember is "things break," and often. Even if you're relatively handy, you can spend $50–$100 per month on repairs. If you're not handy, or if you're living in an older RV, you'll have to revise that number—upwards. This doesn't include your regular vehicle maintenance, like oil changes. We also recommend having an emergency fund of at least $2,000, and we mean emergencies only. Because they do happen.

Don't forget "the dark side" of RV living: you're going to have to dump your waste tanks. Gas stations and travel stations (Pilot/Flying J/Love's) to be the cheapest—and sometimes free. If we pull into an RV park for dumping, we usually pay $10. Of course, if you're staying at an RV park, you can dump for free.

How About Cell Phone and Internet Service?

You will probably want a dependable cell phone and Internet service wherever you go, so scrimping on this is not really an option if you're going to be doing any work on the road. As of this writing, Verizon has the widest network nationally, and they offer an unlimited data plan (with a few small catches). Other companies also offer unlimited service, but there are more 'dead zones' than with Verizon. Either getting a hotspot as a dedicated line or using your cell phone as a Wi-Fi hotspot, you'll rack up the data quickly. Verizon's top-level unlimited price is $95 a month per line. At two phones and a hotspot, that's $285 a month, but most of us can do just fine without a dedicated line for a hotspot, bringing it down to $190. While some RV parks have good reliable free Wi-Fi, it's hit-or-miss. So if you use the Internet for work, or even if you just want to stream a movie on Netflix, you're better off with your own source.

What Will I Spend on Laundry?

Whether you're using the washers and dryers at an RV park or taking your stuff to the laundromat, you're going to have to do your laundry. It costs about $5 per load, figure 2–3 loads per laundry day, and doing laundry 2–3 times per month.

Entertainment—How Much Fun Money?

Here again, it depends on where you're going and what you like to do. Free activities are free, which is great. If you're going to either Disneyland or Disney World, you're going to spend a lot of money. Most expenses are in that big gray area. If you can set aside $250 a month for entertainment, you will never be short of fun—and you don't have to spend it all.

Groceries, Clothes, Etc.

These are things you'd be spending on whether you live in a house or an RV. They shouldn't be too different from your current household budget, as long as you remember something I said earlier: you're not on permanent vacation. Keep shopping in supermarkets, not the camp store at the RV Park. Souvenirs come out of the entertainment budget, even if it's an overpriced t-shirt that says, "I visited West Podunk." Cook or grill more than you eat in restaurants, just as you would if you lived in a house, and you'll be okay.

Decorating An RV

Owning an RV or RV resemble owning a house...a house on wheels. There are numerous ways that you can add your very own taste to your vehicle when you are embarking on enhancing an RV; it's discovering what spending plan you have and to what extent you need to bring with finishing.

The Most Efficient Method to Design an RV

There are numerous shapes and styles to RVs and various approaches to design them. So by what means would you be able to pick a style that will suit who you are? Observing the style of your RV is one crucial element, and another is the amount you will spend. Shouldn't something be said about imagination... can you envision how the RV will look when wrapped up?

Improve an RV

Take a look at how much money it can take to design your RV. If you are after a style that will take your ugly old RV to the "Goodness" component (staggering and stunning), then you should spend up enormous. Shopping at spots that stock quality items and coordinating topics will come into place. You could shade co-ordinate the whole vehicle from the parlor seats to pads, blinds, towels, kitchen adornments, lavatory assistants, and even bedding!! Some most loved hues are Red, Dark, and White. So, to brighten your transport, you could utilize embellishments that match the shading plan of your taste.

Envision a Completed RV

Utilizing creative ability, these shading plans can suit any bus... looking beautician and cutting edge. The transport could have a parlor seat with Red and Dark pads; the kitchen could have a Red Pot and red kitchen embellishments, the shower will coordinate with dark towels/face washers and extras in the same shading subject, the fundamental bed could coordinate with a Donna spread in the dark, with a touch of red. Group it up with white panties all through and again Dark seat tops in the kitchen. Keeping to a basic shading conspire and speaking to them all through the transport will take a plain exhausting old transport to an "Amazing" searching transport when hunting down how to finish an RV.

Time to Brighten an RV

It will require investment to brighten an RV, contingent upon what you need to do and the amount you need to do. If you are shy of time, then you can procure Brightening Organizations, which will come in and listen to your prerequisites, bringing down notes and afterward giving you a quote.

When you are content with the organization and you will spend the cash, enlivening an RV will take a little time for your benefit.

Cherishing Your RV

When you have the creative energy, the time dealt with the cash accessible to spend then cherishing your RV will be the fun piece of enhancement. Inside no time, your RV will turn into a showpiece, and you will be pleased to demonstrate your final results; with sharing your RV to family/companions and even reporters... you could include your RV in Magazines and Daily papers!

The most efficient method to brighten an RV is simple once you know how. Here are a couple of fundamental tips to recollect when you set out to brighten:

- Time - Do you have room schedule-wise, or will you utilize an organization?
- Cash - What amount would you say you will spend?
- Sharing Plan - Discovering what shading you like will make embellishing simpler.
- Creative energy - Would you be able to picture the deciding result?
- Love - Cherishing your design work, and the end image will demonstrate your belongings.

The Pros and Cons of Full-Time RVing

There are any number of benefits to living free and several downsides. For us, the upsides are way better, but both sides need to be considered before embarking on the adventure of a lifetime.

Remember that the benefits and drawbacks do not appear at the start of your journey. Some become part of your routine, some of the benefits and the drawbacks don't even show up until you've been on the road for a year or two. Some, I'm sure we're still looking forward to!

Cons

Let's start with some of the cons first:

Regular Maintenance

Every home needs upkeep, and a home that you drive down the highway at 60 miles an hour is going to need a lot more. Consider that, as heavy as it is; your RV is built as lightweight as possible, so your fixtures and fittings don't have the stability and quality of a non-moving residence. Now add on the fact that your home is also a vehicle with its own set of repair and replacement needs! You'll have to keep up on your scheduled maintenance and be ready for the unforeseen. Keep a maintenance fund in your savings, even if you think everything is under warranty.

Fluctuating Budget

The 9 to 5 housebound life gives you the ability to plan your finances much more carefully than the RV lifestyle. Campgrounds, fuel, unexpected maintenance, and even the freedom to make quick decisions can wreak havoc on any kind of budget. Sometimes keeping careful track of your expenses is the best thing you can do. A budgeting app like Every Dollar can make monthly tracking easy. If you track every single expense (however small), you'll always know where your money is going, make changes, and be able to (partially) plan for your needs.

Internet Frustration

Even with 4G or the upcoming 5G, you will experience plenty of times when your Internet connection and service will be spotty, or worse. A hotspot or two is essential, and even with those, it will not be what you would have in a house. If you're going to work remotely, a cell signal booster like Weboost might do the trick, although they're not cheap. If you're thinking of depending on campground Wi-Fi, you'll find that most of them are disappointing.

Medical Care

Your regular doctors may not be close by. This could be a pro if you use it as motivation to stay healthy!

Weather

You're closer to the weather when you live in an RV, and you'll need to keep track of the daily and weekly forecast. This can be a priority for your safety and the safety of your companions and your RV.

Pros

Now for some of the pros!

New Places, New Experiences

It's a big country. There's a new sight around every bend in the road, people you haven't met yet at every campground, and even the sunsets vary depending on where you are—National parks, beaches, theme parks, forests, historical places, wherever's next. You're the nomad and the navigator. Full-time RVing means no boredom.

You've Got Your Stuff

Vacationers have to pack and usually travel light. And folks who live in a house have all kinds of things stored in the basement or the garage. When you're full-time in your RV, you have more clothing choices, and you know where your things are. You don't forget your toothbrush; all your toiletries are right there. Your storage is limited, so you've got to know where everything is. And you've got all your toys, too! And no matter where you go, you get to sleep in your own bed every night.

Taking It Slow on the Go

When you live on the road, you decide how long to stay. It can be enjoyable to spend a month or two in a new location and take the time to get to know the area and make new friends, to see a town as its residents do before moving on.

Flexibility

It's also fun to be able to leave when you feel like it. Stick to a plan or change the plan at will—you take your home with you, so go whenever you're ready. It's also easier to visit friends and family wherever they live.

Growing Closer

Even though the road is home, you'll still be living in a relatively small space. As close as you and your partner are now, living in full-time VR will teach you things about yourself and the other, which is wonderful and you may never get to experience it.

Transitioning into the RV Lifestyle

Adjusting to Your New Life on the Road

There are a few things you need to remember before you start your journey, as well as certain factors to consider during your journey.

Think About Your Life Before Living It

It does not matter if you are planning to travel alone, with your pets, friends, or family. Having a plan in mind helps you understand what you might need to do with certain components of RV life. Here are some questions for you to consider. You can add as many questions to the list below as you want to get a complete picture of your strategy.

- What are you going to do with your house once you've left? Are you planning to keep it locked, or would you like to entrust it to someone else?
- Do you have a way to earn income while on the road?
- How are you going to stay connected?
- Are you comfortable living in backcountry areas and campgrounds, or are you only looking to stay in 5-star RV resorts?

Work Out a Rough Budget

You need to be aware of what kind of expenses you are going to have while you're traveling. Here, it's time to add in as many details as you would like so that you are completely aware of all the expenses you will incur on your journey.

Living the Lifestyle

You are transitioning from one lifestyle to the next. This means you are still going to have to perform your daily chores, run errands, pay bills, and engage in your usual activities. As a result, you should decide if you like to stay in one place for a long time or move from one area to another on a regular basis. Are you comfortable boondocking out in the national forests, or are you only interested in using campgrounds?

By knowing your travel style, you might gain a better idea of how you will take care of your daily tasks and find time for your work and other projects.

How to Survive Living in a Small Space?

Once you have decided to live in an RV, it is not just about taking care of your daily needs, but also about making the most out of a tiny space. How can one do it? What should one remember when living in such a small area?

Multi-Purpose Spaces

Since you are not going to have a lot of space for everything, you should think about how you are going to use existing surfaces for various purposes. For example, your dining table could serve as your workspace and for preparing your meals.

You might also have to put many items in one spot. Often, you might find that your laptop and work tech will be sharing space with your groceries and other random items. Be prepared for this, and even try to think about ways you can create spaces that can be used for many purposes.

Make Time for the Outdoors

Living in a small space means you are not going to get a lot of natural light. Even if you have windows, you might not receive the required amount of natural light to maintain your health. Take some time to relax outside and take in the scenery. This could also be the perfect time to pick up some healthy habits, such as walking or jogging. Whatever it may be, it will allow you to explore the world outside, get some fresh air, and even flex your muscles.

Besides, you might need to stretch your legs once in a while, so why not do it through an activity?

Learn to Cook Simple Meals

Sometimes, you won't have the opportunity to prepare a fancy five-course meal, especially when you are driving for long hours. This is why it's a good idea to try and learn quick one-pot meals. There are so many options available online to offer you variety, and they don't take too much time to prepare.

However, this does not mean you can never prepare a nice dinner or a wonderful breakfast, but it is better to know how to cook different kinds of meals so you are prepared for any occasion. For example, let's say you are running out of supplies and you still have a day to go before you can restock. By knowing how to cook a nice and simple meal, you can make use of what you have to the fullest.

Traveling with Kids and Animals

To better deal with this, let's split them in two. We are going to first focus on RVing with your kids and then move on to pets.

Tips for RVing with Your Kids

Get the Right RV

This is probably self-explanatory, but make sure your RV is appropriate for your kids. Typically, when you are getting your RV, you will be told how many people the RV is ideal for. Some RVs are good for three to four people, while others give two to seven people a wider option. Knowing this will help you decide which motorhome will give you as much comfort as possible during your travels.

Plan the Trip in Advance

It is fun to be spontaneous, and while you can still do that, it is always better to have a rough plan for your travels. This allows you to determine specific stops for taking a break, having food, using the facilities, restocking certain items, or simply allowing the kids to experience the outdoors for a bit.

Even if you don't want to construct a plan, make sure you have a map or guide that shows where significant places are. These could include gas stations, campgrounds, parks, and other areas for your RV. This way, even if you need to make an emergency stop for any reason, you can quickly refer to your map and find the closest campground or RV spot for your motorhome.

You can even get some incredible RV apps to help you plan your journey or guide you towards the nearest essential spot.

Check Out Some of These Apps

- InRoute Route Planner
- Roadtrippers
- Google Trips

I would also recommend the following navigation app:

- **CoPilot RV:** I like this app since you can actually use it offline! The best part is that you can enter your RV's height and width, and it will calculate the best route to a specific location without running into low bridges or tight tunnels—definitely something that could come in handy if you don't have the best internet connection.

These apps give you added benefits or make your trip more interesting:

- **Gas Buddy:** If you don't just want to know where the nearest gas station is, but where the cheapest one is, then you need this app.
- **TuneIn Radio:** You get to tune in to local radio stations for news or your favorite sport updates.

For finding spots for camping, you can use the below apps:

- Reserve America
- Recreation.gov
- iOverlander
- Campendium

Tips for RVing with Pets

Rules of the Road

While it might seem rather natural to allow your pets to roam around the RV while you are driving, it could actually be dangerous for both you and the pet (and the RV, of course).

While you might be following the speed limits, the same cannot be said about other drivers. You will need to keep your eyes on the road to deal with any troublesome motorists. But even if you are on an empty stretch of road, wandering pets tend to cause distractions, which is something you shouldn't have to worry about when driving.

Pack the Essentials

When in doubt, make a list.

Get all the essentials for your pet. Here is a list I made to give you a little guidance on what you should include, but feel free to modify it as you see fit:

- Leash
- Crates
- Litter
- Toys
- Pet carriers
- Refuse bags for pet droppings
- Brush and grooming items

I understand that many people dislike the idea of transporting their pets to carriers, but consider what is more important: a temporary safe enclosure for your pet or a potential accident waiting to happen?

Update Your Pet IDs and Bring Them with You

As with the list you made during the downsizing process, make sure you get the actual IDs of your pets. Make a few copies and also save them virtually.

Making Your RV Feel Like Home

Home is where the heart is, even it's said home is moving around a lot.

People often wonder if they can make their RV feel a little more like the home they've left behind. It is definitely possible, and I am going to show you how.

Home Tip #1: Change the RV Mattress

The mattress that came with your RV may not be appropriate for you, so make sure you replace it with something more comfortable. If you feel that getting a brand-new mattress is not something you would like to invest in, there are cheaper alternatives. For one, you can get a mattress topper, which is essentially a layer of bedding you add on top of your mattress. Alternatively, you could even take the mattress from your home and put it in your RV if the mattress can fit on the RV's bed.

Home Tip #2: Add Wall Decor

Include pictures, stickers, or other wall decorations to bring a little color and life to your RV. Adding wall clocks showing times from different parts of the world is also a wonderful addition.

Here are some additional suggestions:

- A map of the country or region.
- Photo frames containing fun sayings or messages.
- Hanging pots and plants (make sure they are completely secure, or you could choose artificial plants, as well). HINT: You can choose to take down the pots and plants when you are traveling and set them up again after you have parked your RV, but that means you have to manage your space very well since these decorative items can take up a lot of space.
- LED lights.
- Flameless candles (they set the ambiance without setting your RV on fire).
- Hanging wicker baskets is a great idea for décor and storage.

Home Tip #3: Use Oil Diffuser

Get your RV smelling fresh. It doesn't take too long for the RV to accumulate a plethora of scents from your travels. Using an oil diffuser can make all the difference in the world. Scents such as eucalyptus add a little freshness into the air, while rose can provide a wonderful sweet smell.

Look at different oils and find the one that suits you. If you're traveling with others, let them smell the scents before purchasing them to see if anyone is allergic to the fragrance.

Home Tip #4: Home Comforts

Remember how we talked about bringing bathroom slippers and cutlery? Many people prefer to buy new items for the RV, but I like to have things from my home because they make the RV feel lived in. Bring in your favorite coffee mug. Get your comfortable home slippers. Add your welcome mats if you would like. Before entering your RV, things you have already used have a sense of value and bringing them to your RV transfers that value to your motorhome.

Home Tip #5: Add Curtains

If your RV comes with valences, then see if you can replace them with curtains. With such a simple addition, the interior of your RV transforms into something comfortable and cozy.

What You Need to Know Before You Go

How Do You Dump the Tanks?

Cleaning the RV holding tanks is not a job anyone would willingly take. However, it has to be done, and you have to dispose of the human waste properly (while taking care not to disturb the environment).

There are some simple steps to take care of the tanks, but before we start doing that, let's see what we might need in order to prepare ourselves.

Prepping With the Right Tools

Before you begin dumping anything from your RV, you will need the following tools:

- Disposable gloves.
- Rinse the hose to flush out the black water.
- Bleach wipes for sanitation.
- Clear sewer adaptor.
- Sewer extension hose (ideally 30 feet long).
- Hose elbow.
- Hand sanitizer to clean your hands after you are done.

Types of RV Tanks

Depending on how your RV has been set up, you might find the below tanks attached to your motorhome:

- Black tank to take care of the wastewater and sewage from your toilet
- Gray tank to deal with the water from your shower and sinks
- A freshwater tank that stores clean water (this is the water you use in the shower and sinks)

We are going to start by learning how to empty the black water tank first.

Waste Disposal

Ideally, look for RV dump stations and other designated areas for taking care of the black water tank. These areas and installations are specially made to provide you with the convenience of cleaning out your tanks in a safe, sanitary manner. Once you have located these tanks, follow the process below:

1. Put on your gloves and make sure there are no tears in the fabric. Make sure the valves of the gray and black tanks are closed before you move on to the next step.
2. Now start by attaching one end of the hose to the sewer or dump station hole. You can also make use of a hose elbow and a hose ring to connect the hose properly to the dump station or sewer hole. By doing so, you can attach the hose securely. However, this is not always needed if you are careful when getting rid of the waste. Also, don't just leave your hose lying around when you are draining your RV. Make sure you are either holding it or securing it using the elbow and hose ring.
3. Connect the hose to the black water tank on the other end. You might think that people are cautious when it comes to attaching their hoses, but you'd be surprised at how many people do not double-check to ensure that everything is securely fastened. One way to connect the hose to the tank is by first positioning the opening underneath the black tank outlet. Once done, open the flap and allow any drips to fall directly into the hose.
4. When you're certain that everything is securely fastened, turn on the black tank water valve first. You will hear the noise of wastage rushing through the hose. Eventually, you will start to hear a trickling sound.
5. Do not remove the hose yet. Flush the black tank with water to clean it completely. Certain RVs have the ability to use the clean water from the gray water tank to perform this task. If not, you might have a different setup to help you with this process. Typically, you might also have a rinse system in the RV that you can connect to the black tank.
6. Make sure you close the valve to your black water tank.
7. When you are done, remove the end of the hose that is connected to the tank first. Lift it up so you can drain any leftover materials from the pipe straight down into the dump station or sewer hole. If you have a separate hose for cleaning, use that to clean the hose instead.
8. Finally, detach the end of the hose connected to the dump station or sewer hole.
9. Steps 2 through 8 should be repeated for the gray water tank.

Regular Maintenance on the Road

Just like your tank, your RV is going to need some maintenance as well. To a lot of people, this might seem like an overwhelming task since they are often left wondering what part of the RV they should start working on first.

Here is a list to get you started.

Maintenance #1: Look at the Seams and Seals of the RV

Use your ladder (or some other way) to inspect the roof of your RV. Check for any leakages that could let rainwater into the interior of the vehicle. Check the skylights, vents, edges, and air conditioning unit. If you notice any leaks, you can make use of any number of sealants available in the market. However, try to choose a sealant that works well with the material your RV is made of. Think about getting the gaps or holes fixed sometime in the near future to provide a more long-term solution to the problem.

Maintenance #2: Check Your Tire Pressure and Wheel Nuts

Your RV's tires are going to suffer quite a bit of abuse (not to mention with the weight of the RV on them). Make sure you are checking the air pressure on your wheels to maintain safety on the road. Look at the lug nuts to see if any of them have come loose, even just a little, and make sure the tires are not over-inflated. This could cause them to explode, leading to some serious accidents on the road. The seasons affect the tire pressure, as well.

Maintenance #3: Check the Batteries

Your aim with the batteries is to keep them fully charged, but people don't always pay attention to that, as it means making frequent trips to the garage. However, what you can do is make sure the batteries are in good condition before your long trips.

Why Your RV Needs to Be Level

Often, people don't think about leveling their RV, but this is an important part of taking care of your motorhome. Whether you are looking to camp somewhere temporarily or use the RV as a new home, leveling allows you to take advantage of some of the RV's features.

If you don't level your RV, you might experience one (or all) of the below problems.

Warm Refrigerator

One morning, you wake up to the smell of fresh air. A delicious breakfast would be ideal. So you head out to the refrigerator to get your ingredients. However, as soon as you open the door, you notice the food has spoiled. What's more, the beer is warm as coffee (the horror!).

What just happened? The refrigerator was working perfectly yesterday. In fact, you can still taste the lingering flavor of the nice, chilled beer you were enjoying just last night.

Time for a bit of science. Liquid ammonia flows through a part of the evaporator coils inside the refrigerator, which are usually at low temperatures. But one of the key components to keep this process going is gravity. As you probably already know, liquids don't go uphill (if it does, then you have discovered something magnificent). If your RV is uneven, one side of the refrigerator is tilted upwards, preventing the liquid from reaching that place. The ammonia can actually pool and settle, causing a blockage in your refrigerator.

What to Do If the RV Breaks Down

Spending a night stranded on the side of the road does not contribute to the adventure you had planned for yourself or your family, which is why you should keep the below tips in mind.

Prevention Is Better Than Repair

Make sure you are performing routine maintenance and check-ups on your RV. Do not leave your motorhome unattended for a long time. Through check-ups, you can discover any problem before it worsens. You must be aggressive when you are working on preventive care. It's either that or looking embarrassingly in your side mirror as your RV is billowing smoke through a nice neighborhood and the folks nearby are throwing some rather colorful language your way. In all honesty, a broken-down RV is a danger to you, as well as the people who are in close proximity to the vehicle.

When Trouble Comes Knocking at the Door

In a perfect world, inspections are all it takes to keep trouble at bay, but we are not in a perfect world, and, well, excrement happens (this is strictly a PG-13 book). Here, we are going to assume the inevitable has happened. So what do you do? How can you deal with the scenario?

If a breakdown occurs, it could happen in any form ranging from an empty gas tank to a wobbly wire to other mechanical failures indicated by terrifying noises you know should not be coming out of any vehicle, let alone one you live in. In such cases, if you can keep driving, then do so until you have reached a safe place to park your motorhome, whether that place is a truck shop, RV camp, or wide-open space. During this process, take it slow. Turn on your hazard lights and pull over to the side of the road, allowing traffic to pass. If you start smelling something funky, make sure you find a spot to pull over as quickly as possible.

Electricity and Power

Importance of Power

Essentially, one of the things you should remember when you are thinking about your RV's power is a formula: watts, which signifies the total power, is a result of current, the product of amps and volts. If you transfer the statement into an equation, it's written as watts = amps x volts or W = A x V.

The above formula will help you manage the number of electrical devices you have plugged in at any point in your RV. You could potentially use all the electrical devices you have, as long as they are within the limit of the total wattage. However, if you cross the limit, then you might just trip the circuit. That means interrupting a plot twist in the movie you were watching in the RV—definitely not something you would want to happen.

Read up about the total wattage of your RV. You can find this information in your vehicle's manual. When you are using electrical appliances, check how much power is needed for each appliance. This way, you can find out if you have to turn off some electrical devices before plugging in another. You really don't want your RV to shut down because you were making coffee.

One for Two

Your RV comes with two different types of electrical systems:

- A 12-volt electrical system.
- A 120-volt electrical system.

A single battery typically powers the 12-volt electrical system, but that may not be the case as some RVs have multiple batteries powering the system. This system is responsible for running your refrigerator, your water heater, your water pump, most of the lights in your RV, and many other vital components. The 120-volt electrical system, on the other hand, is used for other devices plugged into outlets, such as the television, kitchen appliances, phone chargers, or computer power cords. A generator usually powers the 120-volt system.

In the end, both systems need to be charged whenever you get the opportunity. But how can you charge them? It all comes down to the power cord.

Part V

—

Boondocking 101

Camping and Boondocking Basics

Campsites for Your RV

Finding the perfect campsite is part of the adventure for many RVers.

When it comes to campsites, everyone has their own preferences—some like them secluded, others like them right next to the fun.

We're going to break down some of the significant campsite types and explain what you can expect at each one.

National Park Service Sites

The National Park Service (NPS) runs more than 1,420 different campgrounds, making this an excellent resource for RV owners.

There is often a fee to use the sites managed by the NPS, and these fees can vary between campgrounds. There is frequently a limit on the time you can camp in your RV at an NPS campground, with an average range of time between about two weeks to two months. Some NPS campgrounds have full hookups with dumping stations, while others simply have the space for a few smaller RVs.

However, many of the best national parks in the US, from Death Valley to Joshua Tree to the Smoky Mountains, have space for you to park your RV and make your home for a while in the thick of some of the planet's best natural space.

The first place to start researching national park campsites is at the official NPS.gov website. This site has detailed information on general NPS rules and sectors on each national park campground and the sites available for RVers.

RV Parks

The other main type of location for RV owners is RV parks.

These are privately owned properties that offer RV parking and access to some or all of the following:

- Swimming pools and other recreational activities.
- Wi-Fi.
- Dump stations.
- Convenience stores.

RV parks come in a variety of configurations, ranging from private to public to state parks. The similarities between these three types are that they all offer a place to park your RV and hookups for water, sewage, and electricity.

Each has its own set of rules and regulations that you should be aware of before signing a contract or handing over money.

However, these types of RV accommodations can be very useful for taking some time off the road and giving your rig a rest from wear and tear while recharging your electrical system, dumping your holding tanks, and performing other necessary maintenance.

These RV parks are much more common than national parks or other similar campsites for your RV, making them a convenience worth considering.

Urban Camping

One unique way to enjoy the RV lifestyle is to embrace an urban area and all the culture, sights and sounds it has to offer.

This type of RV lifestyle gives you easy access to towns and cities with all their modern comforts, while still allowing you to camp in relative safety, sometimes just a few blocks from a police station.

If you are a fan of RV Living but aren't always a fan of the "roughing it" approach that some RVers embrace, finding an RV park within a city—and there are more of those than you might think—may be the proverbial Goldilocks situation for you.

Camping out in your RV in a city can also be a nice change of pace if you want to take in a bit of all the country has to offer.

Boondocking

In the RV world, "boondocking" can have a couple of different meanings, but overall it refers to finding a spot to camp your RV overnight or longer that is not necessarily designed for RVs and doesn't offer the amenities of an RV park or campsites intended for that purpose.

For some RVers, any place to camp with your RV without water, power, or sewage hookups is a type of boondocking. More specifically, staying at this type of campsite is known as "dry camping."

For others, the essence of boondocking is finding a free spot to stay with your RV, "free" being the operative word.

However, what unites all definitions of boondocking is that they all involve staying somewhere not designed specifically for RV camping or parking.

This style of camping requires a bit more planning and safety measures than traditional RV travel. It also requires a fair bit of experience and knowledge about which sites are legal to use and the peculiarities of various kinds of boondocking spots.

Boondocking: Where to Start

Before embarking on your boondocking adventure, you'll need to know exactly where you can go.

There are communities like Campendium, which has a large segment detailing free RV campsites on public lands in North America with the internet.

There is also information about a trickier yet potentially more accessible type of boondocking: staying with your RV in a commercial parking lot—as you would find outside a Walmart or truck stop—overnight.

We'll go through a couple of those basic types of boondocking here.

Boondocking: National Forest Service Sites

The National Forest Service (NFS), a United States government agency in charge of managing the country's forests, is a good place to start.

Unlike the National Park Service, the NFS allows for dispersed camping—this means choosing your spot and setting up camp anywhere in the national forest, as long as you're not within the vicinity of any established campgrounds and at least 100 feet away from any streams or water sources.

The NFS also requests that RVers stay out of the path of established roads while boondocking, which seems like solid advice.

There is a 16 day limit per month for dispersed camping on NFS lands, and the service's Leave No Trace policy dictates that you clean all debris and leave your campsite the same as you found it.

Boondocking on NFS land is very much "backcountry" style camping with no amenities. You'll be responsible for providing all of your water, and the only restroom facilities will be whatever you have in your RV.

While you are likely to find natural water sources such as streams or lakes nearby while boondocking on NFS land, this water is very likely to be unsafe to drink.

Boondocking: Parking Lots

Parking lots abound the world over, especially throughout the US and Canada. Many of them sit mostly or entirely empty overnight, with ostensibly plenty of space for you to park your RV for a few hours of rest.

Of course, it's not that simple when a vast majority of these lots are on private property, with many property owners considering unauthorized access to be trespassing.

While boondocking at a parking lot overnight is often a risky proposition at best, there are some notable exceptions—including one particularly massive discount department store chain.

As a rule, Walmart allows for RV parking in their lots. However, the management, or the security, at a Walmart location, may or may not agree with this policy. The Walmart website suggests asking the store manager beforehand, and local laws against overnight parking may supersede store policy.

Other large chains which are generally friendly towards boondockers include Costco and Cracker Barrel.

RV Clubs and Memberships

I had no idea RV memberships existed until we started RVing. Before retirement, I had no idea full-time RVing was a thing. We decided to go full-time despite having little knowledge or experience in the RV world.

Our intention was not to become RVers. Our goal was to travel to each of the fifty states. Purchasing an RV turned out to be the most cost-effective option. So, four days after our wedding, we bought a fixer-upper on Craigslist, plotted our route, and set out.

Because it took us so long to pack up the RV and hit the road on our first day as RVers, we wouldn't arrive at a campground until after the camp offices closed at 5 p.m. We were immediately confronted with an unexpected problem: how do you check into a campground if no one is there?

The Best RV Club Memberships

Harvest Hosts

Harvest Hosts is a one-night free RV membership that allows campers to park their RV at various wineries, vineyards, breweries, farms, and museums.

Cost

$79 annually (price changed Jan 2019)

Benefits

- "One" free night of camping.
- A good way to meet locals.
- 1000+ locations.

The Problem with Harvest Hosts

You won't have any form of hookups if you park at HH spots. Plus, as part of the Harvest Hosts arrangement, participating business owners will let you stay for one night. Moreover, I can tell you from personal experience that the nicer you are (and the more wine, beer, and other alcoholic beverages you buy), the more likely you are to be allowed to stay longer, particularly during the week or off-season.

Harvest Hosts' earlier owners were extremely rigorous about the one-night rule, but the present owners are considerably more relaxed. So you can stay as long as your host will let you to your fantastic Harvest Hosts site. We've only stayed in one place for three nights.

Are Harvest Hosts worth it?

Harvest Hosts theoretically pays for itself in one night. However, the idea behind HH is that in exchange for patronizing the business, you can camp for free (saving yourself at least $35). Because the majority of the participating HH businesses are wineries, breweries, or farms, this is an excellent opportunity to learn about the area and sample local delicacies.

However, just a few bottles of wine will quickly exceed the cost of a campsite. This isn't the best membership for simply saving money. This isn't the ideal subscription if you're only looking to save money. Your hotel costs will decrease, but your spending will almost certainly increase.

HH is fantastic for meeting new people, visiting a new place, and having a fun night with food and drink!!! (They are so fantastic that they deserve all of the exclamation points!) You can stay at numerous HH sites on the east coast for up to three nights and spend more than $100 on wine tasting, a couple of bottles of local wine, and supper.

Good Sam Club

Good Sam Club is the company's reward program (it's separate from their insurance and roadside help, and it's not the same as a Sam's Club membership).

Cost

- $29 annually.
- $50 for two years.
- $79 for three years.

Benefits

- Up to ten percent off camping fees at participating campgrounds.
- Over 2,400 campgrounds participating.
- Up to ten percent off at Camping World.
- Up to eight cents off the gallon at select Pilot Flying J locations.

The Problem with Good Sam

The camping discount offered by Good Sam is quite minimal. It just costs a few dollars per night, so you'll need to use this membership regularly to recoup your investment. But the correspondence that Good Sam sends is my main gripe with them. There was a TON of mail. All of them are attempting to upsell you on other services, including ones you already use. They send me letters twice a week, attempting to sell me things that I already possess and get me to purchase more. STOP KILLING TREES; I've already given you my money.

Is Good Sam Club Worth It?

Good Sam has changed its perks in recent years. It used to offer a three-cent discount per gallon, but that has now been increased to five cents for gas and eight cents for diesel. They used to provide 30% off Camping World purchases; however, that number has since been reduced to 10%. By staying at a couple of campgrounds and filling up your gas tank at their "select" Pilot Flying J locations. Pilot Flying J sites that they "choose." We've been using Good Sam for years, and I'm not sure we've ever saved more than $50; however, it always pays for itself.

Factors That Affect RV And Camping

Pandemics

It is true to say that pandemics increase activities such as RVing. We saw the evidence of this during the height of the pandemics, where the RV industry saw a great increase during that period. One would have expected this since RVing is a good way to move around in a socially distant way. Inside the moving motorhome are usually all the amenities and technology needed to stay in touch.

Regardless of the increase in the RV lifestyle or the provisions available to RVers, the pandemic has also greatly affected RV and camping as well. Due to the severity and the global nature of the coronavirus pandemic, so many activities that make RV camping exciting have been greatly affected.

Many campsites, for instance, were shut at the height of the pandemic. This means it was difficult for many RVers to get hookups and some important resources they needed. Some campsites have opened but have resources such as swimming pools and playgrounds shut.

If you are in the midst of a pandemic and decide to go RVing, here are a few safety tips to keep you safe:

- **Follow the rules and regulations:** Campground rules are made to keep everyone safe, and it is important you abide by them.
- **Apply preventive measures and be cautious:** When you get too excited, it can be easy to forget the situation on the ground. Do not share personal objects with other people. Avoid contact sports and give a good distance from people you talk to. Also, avoid crowded places and contact spots such as door handles.
- **Carry preventive equipment:** Facemasks, gloves, hand sanitizers, and soaps are necessary to prevent the spread of diseases.

About Crowding

As more people discover the world of RV and camping, crowding in campsites is inevitable. Because of this, you might get disappointed when you find out that your favorite campground is all booked. This happens especially during weekends or popular occasions and holidays. You could end up spending more to book a space in the campground.

To help you tackle this problem:

Do not go to the popular places: There are other interesting campgrounds you can go to and find your peace and quiet rather than putting up with all the noise of crowded campgrounds. Oftentimes, some few popular places might be preventing you from exploring other interesting places. Expand your search to find more camp-grounds you can visit.

Make your bookings early: If you really like to see some special events or visit some of the big campgrounds with so many crowds, then you need to make your bookings early. This is, of course, if you are prepared to handle the loud atmosphere of a crowded campground.

Travel during the relaxed seasons: These are seasons with relaxed traffic. People love traveling in seasons like summer, and this is usually the main cause of crowding during such periods. If you don't want to cope with the crowds, you can travel at a different time of year. Furthermore, all the beautiful places to visit in your RV are usually open to visitors all year. With this, you will get more freedom and flexibility.

RV Sizes

The size of RVs also matters a lot when dealing with some campsites. Some campsites do not have the resources to handle large RVs such as fifth wheels and Class A motorhomes. To avoid being rejected because of the size of your RV, you might need to carry out a thorough finding of the campsites to ensure they are equipped for your RV size.

Survival Tips and Staying Safe while Boondocking

If you're concerned about what can go wrong with boondocking, the answer is everything. Anything that can possibly happen in boondocking is likely to happen and at the most inconvenient time at that, which is why I'm putting so much emphasis on being prepared. The best way to get through any problems on the road is really being over-prepared, having backups for your backups, and thinking thoroughly ahead. That being said, even if we're armed to the teeth with generators, repair tools, and so on, there will inevitably come a time in boondocking when we're completely caught off guard.

If you're wondering what has gone wrong for me in my boondocking adventures, the answer is also just about everything. My van has broken down in the middle of nowhere. I have gotten lost in the middle of the wilderness after camping at a remote site, and I had a nasty tangle with some poison ivy. While I have so far had the sheer luck of always finding people who are welcoming and kind, there are a lot of people out there who don't take well couple boondockers, and solo boondockers especially attract all kinds of crazies. That's why it's important to state that safety should be your foremost goal in any boondocking trip.

Aside from safety issues, there's also the issue of basic survival and what it takes to camp at some of the country's most remote locations. You'll be separated from most of the basic necessities that we take for granted while living in a town or city, and the simple act of knowing where to find water can be a lifesaver. Also, believe it or not, I learned to go fishing, to clean my catch, and to cook the fish while I was boondocking.

Now that I've been boondocking for a few years now, I already have more than a few tricks up my sleeve. But if you're wondering what kind of survival tips I wish I knew back when I was starting out, I can guarantee that there's a long list of that too. Here are the basic survival tips that I wish I knew back when I was a newbie to boondocking.

Basic Survival Tips for Boondocking

1. Navigation

I find it funny that boondockers would pack a solar power system, a backup generator, three propane tanks, and an electric blanket but will forget to bring a simple map and compass. It's fair to say that most vehicles used for boondocking can't really go so much off the grid that the chances of being lost in the wilderness are high, but believe me when I say that it has happened.

The first rule of navigation is paying attention to where you are and where you're going. I would say that 70% of good navigational skills is just knowing which direction you came from and which direction you're going. It's also important to keep a visual map of the terrain and know where you are in relation to an important landmark, like the road or the trail.

If you've never used a map and compass before, then just stick to the basics and keep practicing. Align the map to the north, find where you are using different bearings landmarks, and triangulate your position.

Some simple tips also include knowing which direction the North Star is and using its position to know which direction you're facing. Others include using the full moon to find the true North. There are plenty of natural navigational methods that you can explore more if you're interested.

2. Identifying Dangerous Plants

If you're headed towards a new area, like a state that you've never been to before, it will come in very handy to do a quick internet search on the dangerous plants that populate the place. Trust me when I say that getting the itches from poison ivy while you're camping on a remote site is beyond uncomfortable. By simply familiarizing yourself with any possibly dangerous flora near your potential campsites, you can save yourself a lot of grief.

3. Fishing

It might sound like a hobby more than anything else, but fishing is a great way to get a natural source of food while you're boondocking in a remote area with nearby bodies of water. The majority of people are unaware that all you really need to get started fishing is a hook, a line, and some bait. And the upside of always having some fishing line around? Because it's so sturdy and resilient, you can use it to secure your belongings and maybe even set up some traps if you know how.

4. Finding and Purifying Water

We don't expect you to be a boy scout and learn how to find a fresh water source in the middle of nowhere. However, it's important to always take note of where you can find fresh water when you're choosing your campsites. It's as simple as checking a map or even just asking locals and other boondockers. As for purifying water, it doesn't hurt to have a kettle along for boiling water or some water purifying tabs for good measure.

5. Building a Fire

You would be surprised at how many boondockers I've met suddenly ran out of propane while they were camping at remote spots in the wild. By knowing how to build a fire from kindling and tinder, you can save yourself a lot of grief.

The process is simple enough. Find wood that's so dry they make a cracking sound when you break them. Place the dry wood or kindling underneath, and use dry grass or dry leaves as your tinder. Don't forget to place some rocks around your fire to stop it from potentially spreading. Light the tinder first to start the fire, and then place some of the kindling on top or near the tinder to keep the fire going.

Even if you have matches or lighters with you, it doesn't hurt to have an emergency flint firestarter.

6. Taking Stock of What You've Got

When you're new to a campsite, it never hurts to look around, explore a little, and check your available natural resources. You could have a lot of kindling lying around, or you could have a freshwater brook nearby that you didn't know was there. Just by simply looking around, you'd be surprised at what you'll find that's useful later. Looking around also serves the double purpose of checking for any wildlife or dangerous plants near your camp.

7. Knowing a Few Tricks for Mechanical Repairs

One of the most important skills that I honed and I'm still continuing to hone as I'm boondocking is knowing how to make small mechanical repairs on the road. Believe me when I say that I was completely clueless when it comes to engines and small vehicle repairs when I was just starting out. Thankfully, I have learned a few tricks, and I've now become handier in keeping my vehicle running well.

Dealing with Insects and Animals While Boondocking

Now that you've learned a few basic survival tips that can come in handy while you're boondocking as well as stealth camping, what about dealing with the local wildlife and insects? I'm sure it won't surprise you to know that insects are a very common problem when you're boondocking, and especially when you're stealth camping, but did you know that bears and snakes are just as common?

First, let me give you a few tips on how to deal with mosquitoes and horse flies because those are the ones that seem to bite the most. These concerns are not just for your comfort; they're also for your safety because you can easily get dengue fever while boondocking, and it could pose a serious danger, more so when you're living on the road. It's important to remember that insects and other wildlife carry disease with them, and getting bitten can be dangerous.

Keeping Insects at Bay

The simplest, most straightforward solution to keep mosquitoes and horse flies away is to use mosquito spray like Off mosquito spray. I know no one likes to use Off spray, but they're quite effective in keeping mosquitoes and most other insects away. You can just spray it on your clothes and your shoes, and it will do the trick. If there's really a lot of them, then you're going to have to spray some on your hands and neck as well.

If you noticed, mosquitoes are most active at night and during the early morning, so be sure to use your mosquito spray during that time. If you want good, non-chemical alternatives to mosquito sprays, you can also use herbs like sage, lemon balm, and the citronella plant. Mosquito sprays use the mosquitoes' sense of smell to drive them away, and the same works for these organic alternatives. By just having a citronella plant with you, you can keep mosquitoes away. Horseflies, on the other hand, don't like the smell of eucalyptus and tee tree.

Does that mean you should be carrying herbs and oils around? Not at all. What you can do is invest in a handy diffuser and use these scents to keep insects at bay. You'll have your vehicle smelling great, and you won't have to worry about insect bites, killing two birds with one stone.

Keeping Wildlife at Bay

But what about dealing with wildlife while you're boondocking? The wildlife that you'll encounter will range from small food-stealing squirrels to full-grown black bears. One is a nuisance, and the other one is just terrifying.

Despite the huge size difference between these two examples, the best ways to keep them at bay are pretty similar. One of the best things that you can do to make sure that no weird wildlife comes sniffing around while you're boondocking is to keep the odors of food and supplies at a minimum. That means cleaning up after you're eating and making sure that your trash bags are tight and secure.

It's important to note that it's not only the smell of food that will attract small critters and large ones, like bears. Apparently, they also like the smell of toiletries as well as the scent of common bug sprays like citronella (uh oh!). If you're using mosquito and fly sprays or other organic alternatives, make sure that it stays within your vehicle or its vicinity. If you're using a handy diffuser as I suggested, make sure that its range is not so wide that it can reach any neighboring wildlife. Keep those scents well within the camp.

If you've never heard of bear spray, then now is a good time to know that these handy sprays exist. Keep one or two with you and pray that you never have to use them. I saved mine for when I heard rustling sounds around the camp, and while I did have to use the spray once or twice, I thankfully never encountered a bear while boondocking.

As for snakes, always be careful when you're walking around in high grass or when you're moving logs or pieces of wood. Snakes will generally stay out of your way, but on the off chance that you wander into their territory, they might become aggressive. Always pay close attention to your surroundings, and don't step into areas that you can't see.

Part VI

—

The Emotional Side of RV Living

Emotional Aspects Of RVing

As Mark Twain said we don't have any control over the emotions we feel. They are involuntary.

Since this book is about how to RV on a dime and a dream, my guess is that you have probably more or less already made up your mind that you want to live the RVing lifestyle, but you still have a few nagging concerns from time to time as you think more about the process.

You may be thinking: Will it really work for me, and will I be happy? When you're making this big of a change in your life, there will be a lot of emotions to deal with.

Yes, one big factor to consider when deciding whether to live the RVing lifestyle is the emotional aspect.

One of the biggest emotions you'll have to deal with is the constant gnawing feeling of "What if."

You can analyze all the numbers and the financial part of RVing, but you can't put a number on the emotional part. This is the biggest unknown and probably the scariest part of setting out on living the RVing lifestyle.

Major Emotional Concerns

- Will my family and friends think I've lost my mind? (Some may think you're crazy—others will be sure.)
- Will I get lonely?
- Am I being realistic?
- Will I run out of money?
- Is this a mistake?
- What if my RV breaks down and leaves me stranded?
- What if I get sick?
- Will living 24/7 in a cramped space with my spouse and family drive me crazy?
- If I'm RVing solo, how will I handle living 24/7 by myself—especially if I'm boondocking and not around other people?
- Can I deal with being away from family and friends?

RVing Emotions

The emotions you will have to deal with as an RVer will fall into one of two broad categories—emotions before you hit the road and emotions after you get on the road.

Here are some of the emotions you will be dealing with before you hit the road:

- Selling your house or moving out of your apartment.
- Getting rid of your stuff.
- Dealing with reactions and comments from family and friends.
- Going over and over the numbers and deciding if you can really do it.
- Dealing with all the unknowns.
- The constant "what if" questions in your head.

Maybe keeping the following quotes in mind will help you deal with the unknowns of your RVing adventure.

Emotions You'll Experience after You Get on the Road

- Being away from family and friends.
- Unexpected problems and expenses.
- Will my money run out?
- Did I buy the right RV?
- What if my sources of income dry up?

Feelings to Expect After You Hit the Road

After you get on the road, you'll be questioning yourself for a while. This kind of questioning is normal. The future is unknown, but it is also unknown in your current lifestyle.

Accept that the emotions and doubts you experience when you first begin are normal. When the excitement kicks in, they will fade quickly. How can you be depressed when each day is a new adventure?

Face the fact that leaving your home, job, family, and friends all at once will be a huge emotional challenge. This can be a devastating blow. It can even be frightening. Accept that this is a normal reaction.

Problems Will Arise

Nathan and Marissa (check out their YouTube channel at Less Junk, More Journey) planned for over a year: selling their house, deciding on the right RV for their needs, and getting ready to embark on their full-time RVing journey.

Then they hit the road, and their RV broke down less than 30 minutes after they pulled out. They had to get their RV towed and delay the start of their RVing adventure until the repairs could be made.

My guess is that your luck will be better than theirs, and you will live happily ever after—or at least for more than 30 minutes before you start running into problems.

One Important Thing to Keep in Mind

If you're going to be RVing with someone else, it's important to make sure both parties really want to live the RVing lifestyle.

I've seen it time and time again. One person is gung-ho, and the other person reluctantly goes along with the idea. It can work, and sometimes it does.

I've even seen cases where the reluctant person ends up liking the plan more than the one who originally proposed the idea, but that's not normally the case.

I was talking to a woman last week. She and her husband had been living full time in their 44-foot Class A motorhome for about six months. Her husband had to buy the large 44-foot motorhome before she would even consider living in an RV.

They were from Virginia and were planning on going to Colorado for three months when the "check engine light" came on. It turned out to be a minor annoyance. I believe it was a faulty oxygen sensor.

Anyway, she said, "That's it. We have to get rid of this thing and go back to living in a house. What if we got to Colorado, and that happened?" Their motorhome was only about four years old and in good condition.

Maybe someone should have told her that they have RV repair shops in Colorado.

They should have seriously deliberated the idea before they sold their house and bought a motorhome. And the important thing is that they both should have listened to what the other person was saying and paid attention to what each of them really wanted to do. I'm sure they deliberated it, but my guess is that they each heard what they wanted to hear.

Living in an RV Won't Fix All the Problems in Your Life

If you have emotional baggage, getting out of Dodge won't make it go away.

You will have a lot of emotions to deal with both before and after you hit the road. Look at your emotions as a good thing. They force you to consider all the "what if" thoughts that come to mind.

These need to be considered—and maybe more than once, but at some point, you have to decide that you've considered everything and are prepared to deal with events if and when they happen.

Bottom line: If there were no unknowns, there wouldn't be any adventure. So, embrace the idea that unexpected good things and unexpected bad things are going to happen. Enjoy the adventure.

Why do You Want to Live in an RV?

If you're someone looking to live a life of simplicity or someone who values freedom and minimalism, then living in an RV could be the perfect fit for you. Here we'll explore the benefits and downsides of living in an RV, as well as why it might not be the right choice for everyone.

Whether you want to save money on rent or travel more frequently with less hassle, there are numerous reasons why many people have turned to travel across the country on their own terms. We'll walk through what it's like living in an RV and provide some information about some common issues that those considering a lifestyle change like this will face.

What Is the Housing Situation in California?

First, let's look at the state of California's average rental prices. According to Foreclosure.com, the average rent for a one-bedroom apartment is $1,753 per month. For a two-bedroom apartment, it's $1,968 per month. A two-bedroom condo costs even more at an average of $2,113 per month. To give you an indication of how much you would save on rent if you lived in one of these rental apartments, consider the following:

- In 2016, the median income for a household in California was $61,372.
- According to the US Census Bureau, the national average is $28,560.
- If we compare these numbers to the income, you could potentially save by living in an RV. It's clear that it's a viable option.

The Benefits of a Ranger

Living in an RV might not be perfect for everyone, but there are plenty of reasons why many have made this choice for themselves. Here are some of the benefits of living in an RV that you might want to consider.

1. Less Clutter

When you live in one location for months at a time, it can be easy to accumulate quite a bit of clutter over time. Not only does this clutter keep you from having the freedom to pick up and take off at a moment's notice, but it can also be quite an eyesore.

If you live in an RV, there is no need for you to have anything that you don't use on a daily basis. This is practical since it allows you to bring only the stuff that will enrich your life and eliminate clutter.

2. No Utility Bills

The most appealing aspect of living in an RV is not having to pay rent. If something breaks down or you don't make your payments on time, you won't have to worry about paying bills or having a landlord on your tail.

This is especially true if you want to live in a recreational vehicle (RV) that has public utilities such as water and sewer hookups. More often than not, there are no bills to be paid.

3. No Yard Work

The most important thing I've learned about living in an RV is that you don't have to do yard work at all. If you choose to stay put and just park your RV on the street where it's perfectly legal, you won't have any reason to mow the grass, weed, or otherwise, keep your space neat and tidy.

Looking at the big picture, the cost of living rent-free and not having to do yard work has motivated me personally to make the plunge into RV living.

4. Freedom

When you're paying rent for your apartment, you have a certain amount of freedom in your life. But when you're paying $1,753 per month for that apartment, it would be hard to do any traveling or even take a few days off from work without feeling really guilty about it.

Living in an RV can allow you more freedom in your life if you want to save money and don't have a profession that demands you to be present at all times.

5. The Ability to Work Anywhere

One of the most appealing aspects of working from home is the ability to work at your own pace. You can get up at 4 AM, you can take a break at 10 PM, and you don't have to worry about rescheduling meetings or calling into the office when there's an emergency.

Working from home also means that you don't have to commute daily; it makes life a whole lot easier and more enjoyable.

If you want the ability to work from anywhere in the country, then living in an RV is not only possible but is also quite common among those who want this privilege. There are many jobs available online that will allow you to earn money wherever you are.

6. No Lawn to Mow

I know what you're thinking, and yes, it's absolutely possible to live in an RV without mowing the lawn.

7. No Responsibilities

Many people have realized that life is too short to have so many responsibilities.

If you've felt like you have too many responsibilities that demand your attention on a daily basis, then living in an RV could make a massive difference in your mindset.

8. In Your Neighborhood, There Are a Variety of People with a Variety of Interests

Living in the same city for years at a time can become monotonous for some people if there are no new people to meet with different hobbies or groups of friends to socialize with on a regular basis.

Living in an RV can be a good experience if you live in a location that is full of different people with different hobbies.

9. Freedom from Credit Card Debt

Rent is automatically deducted from your paycheck before it is deposited into your bank account if you live in an apartment or condo. This creates a cycle of constantly having money taken out of your bank account each month to pay for rent and utilities: the more money you pay into the rental unit, the less money you have leftover to do anything else. If your rent payment is delinquent, there's no way to avoid evictions or other unpleasant things that can hurt your credit score.

But with an RV, you don't have to worry about paying rent each month.

10. Space for Your Stuff

When you live in an apartment or condo, there is often not enough room for all of your stuff. Whether you're a packrat or just really like hoarding stuff, it's easy to see how living in one location can lead to clutter and a lack of storage for all of your possessions.

But if you choose to live in an RV instead, there will be no limits on the space that you're able to use for storing all your belongings. The flexibility this provides is incredible!

Is Fear Holding You Back?

If you've always wanted to live full-time in an RV but haven't, I'm guessing fear is holding you back. It isn't the money (though it could be the fear of running out of money).

The prospect of taking a risk elicits feelings of dread. It's a perfectly normal and natural reaction. Fear keeps us safe, but it is all too easy to let fear have more control over our actions than is necessary.

Arming yourself with knowledge and information is one of the most effective ways to overcome fear. The more info you have about a situation, the less fear you will have in making a decision.

That's what I believe you're doing by reading this book. You are receiving the information you require making an informed decision and put it into action.

Another way to overcome fear is to do whatever it is you're afraid of. I remember the first time I was driving my 34-foot Class A motorhome all the way across Atlanta, and I was towing a car with the front wheels on a dolly.

About the time, I was ready to breathe a sigh of relief because I was almost through Atlanta, I made a wrong turn and ended up back downtown, and I had to do it all over again. It was scary, but I made it.

An even worse driving experience for me was driving my motorhome with my car in tow through the narrow streets of downtown St. Augustine, Florida. I think those streets were just barely wide enough for a horse and buggy. But, again, I made it.

After you've done something once, it doesn't seem as scary. That's why I say doing something is a good way to overcome the fear of doing it.

Fear Shows Up in Many Forms

The fear of being hurt, which is why we didn't want to jump off the high diving board as kids, is not the fear you're dealing with here. You don't think you'll get hurt if you start living the RV lifestyle.

Here are some of the most prevalent worries people experience (even though you may not want to admit all of them).

- Fear that your friends will think you're completely irresponsible.
- Fear that you'll run out of money.
- Fear that you won't like the lifestyle and then have to admit that you were wrong.
- Fear of embarrassment if things don't work out.
- Fear of being assaulted when you're RVing by yourself.

My guess is that your greatest fear is that you won't be able to earn the money needed to make it work, that it won't work out and that you'll have to listen to your family and friends say, "I told you so." Even if they don't say it, you can bet they're thinking it.

Most people do not want to admit it, but these are the concerns that prevent many people from living full-time in an RV.

Keep reading, and I'll show you how you can be convinced that you really can make it work and how you can live in your RV on a dime and a dream. After all, that's what the title of the book promised, so keep reading and let me prove to you that you can do it.

Something to Think About

There's an old saying meant to remind you that you don't have to get involved with other people's drama.

The saying is, "It's not my circus and not my monkeys." Sometimes it's good to keep that saying in mind.

But What If You Look at Your Life and Realize That This Is Your Circus, and Those Are Your Monkeys?

In other words, this is your life, and it's going to continue just as it is unless you make some changes.

Does This Describe Your Present Life?

The alarm goes off, and you hurry through your morning (since you didn't want to get up any earlier than necessary). You rush to get ready for work, eat some excuse for breakfast, and grab a cup of coffee to take with you as you head out the door for your commute to work.

You watch the clock all day, wanting to go home, and then the next morning, it's lather, rinse, repeat.

This routine might be okay if you were getting ahead, but are you any better off now than you were last year at this time? How much more money have you saved in the last year?

Making a Change Involves Taking a Risk

A lot of people land a decent job and ride it until they retire. That's the safe way to live life. That may be what you've been doing up to this point, but is it something you want to do for the rest of your life, or would you rather take a chance and try something new?

How many people do you know who thought their job was secure until they went to work one day and found out that it wasn't? It's something to think about. In other words, how much security do you really have?

Whether you're 27, 72, or somewhere in between, you can start now and live a totally different life.

Maybe you don't want a totally different life; you only want a slightly different life. For example, you want to keep your dog (and maybe your spouse), but you would like to see almost everything else changes.

Until recently, quitting your job and living full-time in an RV was not a viable option for most people, but technology (and a variety of other factors) has changed all of that.

That's one of the reasons more than 1,000 new RVs a day are being sold.

It's no longer a question of whether you'll be able to afford to quit your work and live full-time in an RV. The only question is, "Do you really want to?"

Later in this book, I'll convince you that you can afford to do it, but, for now, take my word for it.

RV Living Can be Inexpensive

Living in an RV can be inexpensive because campsites can be free, and power (with the help of solar) can also be free. Basically, you'll need to pay for food, insurance, a few personal items, and that's it. That's the bare minimum, but you'll probably want to spend a little more.

I'll get into all of that later in the book.

I don't mean you have to sit at your desk and work on your computer (although that's one option).

Employers now recognize RVers as being hard-working, dependable employees. They're eager to hire them. For example, Amazon hires thousands of RVers, paying them a good salary and providing them with a free place to camp in order to have them work during October, November, and December to help meet the Christmas demand.

Almost all campgrounds (along with state and federal parks) hire RVers to work a few hours a week in exchange for free camping and usually a small salary.

Lots of other income-producing opportunities for RVers will be described later in the book.

The Risk of Change

I have lived full time in my motorhome for six years now. Before that, I lived in Costa Rica for six months.

There are so many interesting lifestyles out there to choose from. You don't have to stick with just one—I didn't. In fact, I've already made arrangements to go back to Costa Rica to live for a few months in the spring of 2019. (Not in my motorhome, of course.)

Most people think they're locked in the way they're living now.

Society and advertising have brainwashed most of us into believing that we need to keep working, accumulating more stuff, taking a two-week vacation every year (when we can afford it), and being happy.

Most people have a reasonably new car or two (with payments), and they think they've achieved the American Dream.

I think you've about decided that there must be more to life than this and that's why you're reading this book.

You want to know if you have options and, if so, how you can turn them into reality.

As you read the book, you will discover that there is a whole new world out there waiting for you. You'll discover what it's like to live full-time in an RV. You'll learn what it's like to live full-time in an RV. You'll also learn how you can afford to live this lifestyle while putting more money in savings every year than you're doing now.

One final thought: You can't plan everything regardless of how much time you take getting everything ready for your RVing adventure. When I was in engineering school, almost all of my time was spent learning how to design things. But, once I started working as an engineer, I discovered that I spent far more time testing designs than I did designing them. I found out that's the way engineering works. In school, I don't remember ever testing anything.

You've planned everything. Your testing will start when you hit the road.

You can't plan for everything. Well, actually, you can. It's called an emergency fund.

There may be valid reasons why you can't live full-time in an RV right now (aging parents to care for, a business or house to sell, etc.), but fear should not be one of them. Fear is useful to help you make sure you've looked at all of the factors involved, but it shouldn't be a reason not to take the plunge.

Solo RVing done Right

Solo RVing Tips

Will I be alone? How am I going to set everything up on my own? Will it be safe on the road? Will I be on the road a lot? What about my security? These are just some of the questions that will pop into your head if you are thinking about solo RVing. Well, don't you worry because we have certain tips that you can use to ensure that your solo RVing journey is enjoyable!

Design Your Own Adventure

Perhaps the most important benefit of solo RVing is that you have the freedom to create your own adventure. You can decide the route, destination, and activities you want to do once you reach there. When you are traveling by yourself, there are plenty of options, and you don't have to compromise! If you are interested in making a pit stop on the way, then feel free to do so! If you want to stay for an extra night at a campground, then you can do that too! You can create your itinerary as you go along.

Plenty of Research

Before you think about a solo RV trip, you must do plenty of research. You need to research the routes you want to take and also look up the things you can expect along the way, like the campgrounds, towns you will pass through, gas stations, and weigh stations. Learn about how the RV works and ensure that it is properly serviced. Learn about certain essential repairs like fixing a flat tire or replacing a broken light. Make it a point that your gas tank is at least half full and carry some extra fuel with you. Apart from this, keep a couple of numbers for roadside assistance service handy.

Regularly Check-in

Keep your phone charged and keep checking in with your loved ones regularly. Keep sending them constant updates about where you are, the route you are traveling on, and where you are headed. Apart from this, you must bring along an emergency tracker (so that you can be easily found in case of an emergency), a booster signal, and a satellite phone. You should also carry your ID with you at all times and keep a photocopy of all essential documents like insurance, registration documents of the RV, and your driver's license with someone you trust.

Never Advertise That You Are on Your Own

You will certainly be curious and excited to meet new people while traveling, but it is good to be a little cautious. Never give away that you are alone, especially when you have just met someone. Show some prudence when interacting with others and let your instincts guide you.

Arriving Early

Since you are traveling by yourself, regardless of where you are headed, ensure that you always reach your destination when there is some daylight and not when it is pitch dark. Make sure that the office staff is still present at the RV Park or campground by the time you arrive. Make a list of places you plan on visiting or staying in and send this list to your family or anyone you think is right so they can keep tabs on you.

If You Follow These Simple Tips, You'll Be Fine on the Road!

Managing a Relationship with Limited Space

If you are traveling with someone, then there are certain things that you must keep in mind so that the journey doesn't become unpleasant. It can be quite tricky to handle relationships given the space constraint. You will be sharing limited space with your partner while traveling, so it is essential that you learn to manage things. The following are the specific pointers to help you along the way.

Don't Stay Hungry

Hanger is a real thing, and it can be the cause for a lot of bickering. A timely snack will prevent your emotions from getting the best of you. You will certainly be able to think better on a full stomach. Keep a couple of snacks handy at all times. In fact, a lot of full-time RVers traveling with their partners think that hanger is one of the leading causes of unnecessary arguments.

Redefining Intimacy

Since you will be sharing the RV with someone else, you need to learn to redefine romance. You don't need to make any elaborate gestures. In fact, doing something as simple as brewing a pot of coffee in the morning and doing the laundry can be quite romantic too! It certainly isn't a fairytale idea of romance, but remember that full-time RVing isn't a full-blown vacation, and there will be chores that you must do. Learn to appreciate all the little things your partner does.

Managing Your Expectations

Social media can lead you to believe that full-time RVing is all rainbows and unicorns, but keep in mind that you are seeing someone else's version of edited reality. Learn to manage your expectations. If you have bookmarks of all the places you want to visit, then don't have any expectations until you see the place for yourself. Expectations often lead to disappointments, and this, in turn, can lead to unnecessary unpleasantness. Instead, having little or even no expectations might pleasantly surprise you.

Establishing a Routine

Space constraint in an RV is quite real. So, it is a good idea to establish a routine and assign roles! If you cook, then your partner can clean and so on. You both cannot be cooking and cleaning at the same time. If you do this, you will both be merely getting in each other's ways, and things will not get done. Also, establishing a routine brings a level of comfort with it.

Finding Your Tribe

You can always connect with other RVers and can form your own traveling tribe. Also, doing this will make you enjoy the alone time you get with your partner.

Keep Track of Your Finances

Money is a touchy topic, and therefore, it is important that you stay clear and open about your finances. You don't have to be stingy, but it is a good idea to keep track of your expenses and savings. Full-time RVing doesn't mean instant savings, and there will still be some bills that need to be paid.

Learn to Let Go

Learn to let go of minor squabbles and misunderstandings. Take a moment to compose yourself before you say anything, and this can save you from a world of unnecessary grief. Also, you must learn to compromise. There will be certain things that your partner might want to do, and you might not want to. Learn to compromise and find some middle ground. Learning to compromise is essential for any relationship to work and traveling together is no exception. At times, it can be quite enthralling to step out of your comfort zone and explore things.

Start Communicating

Remember that you are stuck with someone else in a small space for prolonged periods. This is quite different from living together at home where you can go to work, come back in the evening, spend some time together and then go to sleep. Full-time RVing means that you are stuck with someone in close quarters all the time! Start communicating openly and honestly. In fact, this is essential to make any relationship work.

Time Out

You must take some time out for yourself. It can be something as simple as going on a leisurely stroll or even sitting on a lawn. You will need some time to recharge yourself.

Decorating Your RV So It Feels Like Home

A significant benefit of traveling in an RV is that you can always have all the amenities you have at home with you while on the road. Road trips become quite enjoyable when it feels like you are traveling while sitting in the comfort of your living room. Here are a couple of simple ways in which you can transform your RV into a home on wheels within no time and without much of a hassle.

Wall Décor

Perhaps the simplest way in which you can personalize any space is by adding some wall décor. The things that you can use for wall décor include photographs of your loved ones, inspiring quotes, photographs of the places you have visited or want to visit, some posters, and so on. You can hang up anything that makes you feel good. You can do all this without worrying about drilling holes into the walls of your RV by using command hooks, Velcro, and even some putty. Another simple option at your disposal these days is to use wall decals.

Add Some Rugs

Most RVs have laminate flooring that is quite easy to clean and maintain; however, a bare, cold hard floor isn't quite welcoming, especially if you plan on living in the RV. So, adding a couple of rugs to the floor is a simple way to fix this. Place a rug near your couch; add runners to your living space, a mat near your bathroom door, and so on. You can quickly add some color and texture to your RV with rugs.

Put Up Some Curtains

A valance makes the RV feel less like home and more like a vehicle. So, add some curtains and the space will look quite welcoming. You can use adjustable curtain rods for this; however, finding curtains of the desired length might not be easy. So, you merely need to purchase regular curtains and then alter them accordingly to meet your requirements. If your RV has a lot of windows, putting curtains on all of them isn't a good idea because it will make the space appear smaller and more crowded. It would be preferable if you chose light-colored curtains, and you will need a staple gun to attach them to the valances.

Add Some Blankets and Throw Pillows

Adding blankets to the bed along with some throw pillows automatically makes the bed seem quite cozy and relaxing. If you have a couch in the RV, then add some throw pillows to it as well. This is a subtle way of adding color and texture to the living space that can make a big difference in making the RV feel like a home.

Painting the Walls and Cabinets

This certainly is a bigger project than prior ideas. If you go ahead with this, then you will be able to transform the entire look of the RV's interior. Painting the walls and cabinets white will make the space seem airier and spacious. You can paint the walls and cabinets according to your preferences. Sticking to neutral and light colors for the walls and opting for hues of rich brown for the cabinets is a good idea.

Apart from all this, please ensure that you always keep the RV clean and clutter-free to make it more welcoming. Use the tips given in here to transform your RV into a home!

Part VII

—

Health, Kitchen Organization, and Safety Tips

Stocking Your RV Vehicle

One thing you must take note of before stocking your RV vehicle is the Gross Vehicle Weight Rating that helps you know the maximum weight your vehicle can carry. To check the weight of your loaded RV, you could use a public scale, look in the yellow pages, or use a local moving van's scale at a fee to check. Ensure that you get the reading for each wheel and that for a trailer, the tongue weight is the weight the trailer coupling puts on the tow hitch.

To know if your vehicle is overloaded, subtract the unloaded vehicle weight from the total weight. That will give you the water's weight in the tanks, the people in the seats, the awnings, the generator, the air conditioners, and other facilities on board. If the figure you get is more than the Gross Vehicle Weight Rating, your vehicle is overloaded. Overloading your vehicle means that your driving costs will get higher and that you are posing a serious risk to your vehicle.

You should also ensure that you distribute your load evenly in the truck. The heavy items should be placed above or in front of the rear axle rather than behind it. The holding tanks are usually located behind the rear axle. Heavy items stored behind the rear axle usually cause the front of the vehicle to lift or the rear end to get dragged when you turn into service stations.

Stocking in the Optional Essentials

- Binoculars: This device is something you should have with you as it helps you see a great distance ahead. You can easily say if you need to be in the right or left lane in cases where you have to access or exit the interstate. It can also help you when you are looking for certain addresses.
- Artificial grass cloth or large mats to be spread beneath picnic tables and around the recreational vehicle entrance. This mat will prevent sand from getting into the vehicle after you work your boots in muddy areas.
- Foldable and outdoor chairs are other things that you must consider getting as an RV vacationer. Some campgrounds don't provide outdoor furniture for their campers, so you might have to get one. Foldable tables are also platforms on which you can have snacks, drinks, and even lunch.
- Grills are necessary for outdoor cooking. Some campgrounds offer grills, but then, most times, they are usually rusty and dirty, so you might not want to place your food directly on them. Propane stoves are easier to clean to use than matches.
- Small whisk brooms will help brush the tables and seats, a plastic tablecloth held down with clamps, and a plastic bench cover with a tie-on to secure it.
- Office supplies are usually stacked in the drawers of the bedroom desk.

- Games and puzzles for camping days.

Your Vacation Budget

Taking a vacation in an RV vehicle needs you to consider a few factors. The cost of transportation usually includes renting or buying an RV, filing the gas, and maintaining the vehicle. These things remain one of the biggest things that could eat deeply into your pockets. The amount of money you spend purchasing gas depends on the amount of time you plan to spend on the road.

If you decide to spend some days hiking, fishing, or on some other local sightseeing, you will be able to save a lot of gas money. The cost you spend on maintaining your vehicle depends on the type of RV vehicle you have. Most RV vehicle rentals are usually in good condition when you get them, so you might not have to spend so much money to get them in the right condition. When traveling on back roads, ensure that you stay away from toll roads that charge fees based on your rig's number of axles. For most RV drivers, the parking charges could get doubled or tripled, even!

RV Rentals

When do you have to rent?

- When you set out on your very first RV journey.
- When you want to replace your current RV with another type.
- When you want to take your family on a two-week vacation once a year.
- When you want to travel for several weeks from a place that is far from home.
- When you want to drive along a rough or rugged stretch of road without having to subject your RV vehicle to wear and tear.
- When you want to travel a long haul, and in only one direction.

How Can You Rent?

There are several companies out there that rent out RVs, so that shouldn't be a problem. The prices usually start at 85 dollars per week. Rental rates do not usually bracket the following:

- **Generator usage:** Generators are only needed if you want to operate air conditioners, microwaves, ovens, and televisions in campgrounds with no electrical hookups. So, when you return the RV vehicle, the dealer would read the generator counter to know how much you logged.
- **Furnishings:** Some RV rental companies offer a few furnishings, like beddings, towels, dishes, cooking pots, and utensils, for meager amounts. Some additional ones include power cords, hoses, plastic trash bags, toilet chemicals, and troubleshooting guides.

- **Connections for travel trailers:** For most companies that rent travel trailers, you might have to furnish your tow vehicle, hitch, and electrical hookups on the tow vehicles.

How to Get the Best Rental Rate?

- Check the prices with several rental companies before you settle for any vehicle. Ensure that you can establish what exactly the lowest priced rental includes, such as free miles, price per mile, amenities such as dishes and linens, etc.
- Try to plan out your trip during the off-season session or some period between the most popular and the least popular travel times. The times of year for these seasons vary depending on the area you are renting.
- Find out in advance whether or not your own automobile insurance agent covers your rental insurance for an RV. Usually, your agent should be able to provide rates cheaper than the rental company.
- Try to plan your trips in loop trips while ensuring that the rental agencies serve as the starting and ending point so that you can avoid the drop-off charges.
- Negotiate based on selection. The more RV vehicles a rental vehicle has, the wider your range of choices will be.

Food and Staying Healthy

Preparing and cooking meals in a vehicle while traveling on the road can be a difficult process. The difference is in your attitude and how easy you make it. Let's take a look at how you can prepare food while traveling.

Cooking and preparing food while on the road requires some adjustments, but you will find it quite easy to prepare food and eat on the road once you make these changes. The galley of an RV is different from the cooking area in a home, and in a van, you won't even have a cooking area.

In addition, you'll often have to use propane for your cooking, which requires you to adapt your timing since it burns hotter than an electric one. Even when you adapt to these differences, you will still have to prepare for some limitations in the types of meals you prepare.

Stocking Food

Since you are going to have less room for food, it is important you shop carefully. Consider the following tips when considering what to buy and how to stock your food:

- A small freezer won't hold much frozen food.
- Large bottles of milk or soda will take up space in a small refrigerator.
- Bulky vegetables won't often fit in refrigerator bins.
- Small items will often slide off the shelves when the vehicle is moving.
- Too many fresh foods will spoil before they are eaten.
- Liquid items will often spill.

It is best to store food in unbreakable plastic containers that can be easily stacked.

There are thirteen tips that can help make it easier for you to prepare and store food:

- Use an under-the-cabinet coffee pot to heat water that can be used to make hot drinks, instant oatmeal, instant mashed potatoes, soups, and other foods.
- You can fill the coffee pot in the morning with hot water and then use it throughout the day, so you don't have to constantly use the generator.
- Pull freezer items out in the morning so they are thawed out by dinnertime.
- If you are going to drive for a long time, have a few frozen dinners on hand for a fast meal.
- Keep a supply of dry nonfat milk on hand, so you always have milk available for when you need it.
- Have meats on hand that can be thawed quickly when necessary.
- Rather than baking, it is cheaper, cleaner, and easier to buy baked goods.

- Having fresh, frozen, or canned fruits and vegetables will provide quick desserts and side dishes.
- Save leftovers, when possible, for lunch.
- Keep bread and cakes in the oven since it keeps them moist and reduces space.
- Have a supply of crackers and cheese since they are good for snacks.
- Avoid grills since they are bulky to store and difficult to clean.
- Use paper plants and plastic utensils on travel days to eliminate cleanup and time.

Food Preparation

When it comes to preparing food on the road, you can do a few things to make it easier. First, you should consider a raw diet. You won't have to cook, wash dishes, refrigerate, or carry pans and pots with this. This is also an inexpensive and healthy alternative.

You can still eat a variety of fruits, vegetables, nuts, and seeds. In addition, some claim that cooking will kill the enzymes in food essential to good health.

Another option is to stick to basic and straightforward cooking methods. This option is good for those living in a van or a smaller RV. With a small propane or butane stove and some safety measures, this can be a great option for those traveling in a van.

If you are living in a van, the biggest issue is a lack of refrigeration. This can often be simply solved by buying the perishable foods you need on the day you are going to cook and doing so in smaller portions that you don't have leftovers. It can be a good idea to travel in a cooler. It is best to buy a 5-day or extreme cooler. Another option is to get a small 12-volt compressor fridge.

Another thing to consider when it comes to storage space is your pots, pans, and utensils. For basic cooking, you won't need much. Often a single, three-quart pot can be used to cook canned foods and spaghetti while also being big enough to fry food as well.

Also, consider a griddle for when you need to cook for larger groups. Utensils are minimal, consisting of a spatula, can opener, knives, forks, spoons, and a couple of plates and bowls.

Cooking Methods on the Road

Now that we have the supplies and organization down, let's consider how you can cook while traveling. An excellent option that works for most travelers is the pressure cooker. An oven is also a great option since it has multiple cooking options with low cost and size.

You basically need to look at your own circumstances and determine what cooking methods work for your living and eating needs. Now that we have the basics of cooking down, let's look at how you can stay clean and healthy while living on the road.

Staying Healthy and Clean

Another common question people have when considering living on the road is how to stay clean. In an RV, this isn't too difficult since there is a fully self-contained system with running hot and cold water as well as bath facilities. However, in a van, it can be more difficult, but not impossible.

Most of the time, the main question is, how do you shower? Although this brings up the definition of a shower. If you are talking about standing under hot water, the answer is different from those who simply want to have a clean body.

You can easily clean yourself by putting water in a basin with mild soap and then wash all of your body with a washcloth. Then you rinse with a soap-free washcloth. Consider the following tips to help yourself stay clean while living on the road:

- Wash frequently - Rather than getting one big shower, you need to keep yourself clean throughout the day.
- Wash up at public restrooms - Carry a washcloth in a Ziploc or use facial cleansing pads.
- Use portable diaper wipes to clean after you go to the bathroom.
- Carry a small bottle of alcohol antibacterial gel to clean when you don't have any visible dirt on your hands.
- Consider using an antibacterial soap such as Palmolive dish soap so you can double up your use.
- Make sure you have enough washcloths on hand to last at least 14 days since you may not do the laundry that often.
- If you don't want to bring a large basin with you, you can wet and rinse in hard-to-reach places with a spray bottle.
- If you want to shower, consider using a solar water bag to get yourself some warm water.
- Always wash your feet separately to avoid fungus.
- Consider washing your hair in a public washroom. Or, if this isn't possible, you can use a large basin or spray bottle. After wetting your hair, you can lather and then rinse with the inlet or spray bottle. It can be a good idea to keep your hair cut short, so there is less to wash.

It isn't that hard to set up a shower if you really need to shower; the main issue is having the room. Simply hook up a shower bag, stand in a large tub and open the spigot to shower. However, remember to conserve water. So you might want to wet down with a spray bottle, lather, and then rinse with the shower bag.

Alternately, if you can't shower in your vehicle and have no place outside to set up a shower, then you can consider some public locations that may offer shower facilities:

- YMCA
- College campuses

- Truck stops
- Gyms
- Public pools or beaches
- Laundromats
- RV parks

Living in a moving vehicle can make staying clean more difficult, but it is not impossible. With a little ingenuity and adjustment, you can stay clean and healthy while living on the road.

We've covered all the basics you need to know and do on the road. However, living on the road means reducing your cost of living and getting the freedom to enjoy life. So let's take a moment to consider how you can find free and cheap entertainment while living on the road.

Health Care on the Road

If you are not old enough to be on Medicare, then it may be a little tricky to find a suitable health plan that can cover you while you are on the road. Since the fate of the ACA (Affordable Care Act) is not looking good, but that was a great option for people like us who wanted coverage and didn't have to worry about finding a doctor or a hospital in or out of network. But I am sure our government will come up with something even better soon.

In the meantime, shop around for a policy that is not HMP but has a PPO option where you can go to almost any doctor or hospital and not have to worry about being out of network.

Outdoor Kitchen Organization Tips, Tricks, and Essential Items

Whenever we see a tour of someone's RV in a video, they always show all their cutlery and plates, cups, etc., neatly tucked in a cupboard and drawer. It always amazes me that this is how they organize their camping kitchen.

The kitchen in any reasonably sized RV is super small. The counter space in my 30-foot trailer is about 8 inches, which is barely enough room to make tea, let alone an entire meal.

I realize that if you have a 45-foot fifth wheel with eight slides, you will have an island and 35 feet of counter space, where you make daily buffets for your party of 15. But for the common folk, that is not the case.

As a rule, we do NOT make meals in the trailer. We make all meals outside. What if it is raining, you ask? Then we either make the meal under a canopy or tarps, or we just say, screw it and eat out that meal.

There Are Many Advantages to Making All Meals Outside

First, this leads to less mess in the trailer. We're looking at spills, crumbs and trying to navigate on multiple surface areas inside the RV. Instead, I clean up by washing the tables, rinsing them off, and turning them on their side for 5 seconds to drain them off.

Second, it gives you more space to work. I have 8 feet of outside counter space using both tables. That beats 8 inches of counter space any day of the week. I am not a super chef who can make 4 different dishes in the space of a breadbox. I need room to move, chop, mix. My trailer kitchen stores food but is not the ideal place for my prep work.

Third, since we also eat outside, it is closer to our "dining area." Eating in a trailer at the dinette is not preferable. Unless you are camping in a bubble, you will be sweeping out the dirt daily, if not more often, and using a flat mop at least once a day as well. The less frequently you need to clean the floor, the better. This is, after all, supposed to be an enjoyable trip, where you do more than just clean 200 square feet 9 times a day.

If we are not prepping inside, it means that we need to have an outdoor kitchen. This is how we set up ours to be as functional as possible.

a) Collapsible tables for food prep. I personally use two tables. Each table is four feet long. The legs fold down, and they cost about $50 each. They are stored stacked in the trailer on travel days. I make them into an "L" formation and use one for meal prep and one for temporary food storage.
b) If you are staying at a campsite or RV park with tighter spacing, you could put the tables up against the trailer, and if it is a really tight site, use one table instead of 2.
c) Clear plastic containers with lids for plates and cups. While your trailer looks sparkling clean in the showroom, remember that you are moving your trailer to a location full of dirt, bugs, and more dirt. I got my containers from the Dollar Store. They are about 10 inches by 18 inches. One holds cups, and one holds plates. I chose see-thru plastic to make it easy to see, which put a label on the top and side of the box to make it super clear. I use another smaller plastic container for larger utensils, such as a ladle, spatula, peeler, large knife, cheese grater, and such.
d) Cutlery Plastic Cases. I have used children's pencil cases (the rectangular ones with a flip-over lid) or smaller plastic containers with a lid (both from the Dollar Store, yes there is a cheap solution theme here) cutlery. Again, we use two containers. I sort them with one for knives and one for fork and spoons. I am not in the mood to stop and clean cutlery halfway through the process, so I bring a dozen or more of each cutlery type, which takes up space and can cram one container too full. Also, it's easier to find an item that way.

The need for reasonable-sized plastic containers cannot be understated if you plan to do your cooking outdoors. When we arrive, we take all the boxes out at the same time and put them on a table. We often leave them on the picnic table between uses since everything is clean and protected from the elements, thanks to the lids

One caveat is if you are camping in a place where you don't trust the neighbors not to help themselves with your stuff while you are away. Then, obviously, bring in the collection when not in use. It still only takes seconds to move the stack in and out of the trailer when needed if you feel more comfortable bringing it in between meals.

e) BBQ. If you have a newer trailer with the built-in BBQ, you are already set. If not, you need to get a tabletop or collapsible BBQ. We have a small folding table to hold our BBQ. You can also use your picnic table, but then you lose space for eating.

The BBQ is used for almost all meals. It is basically a substitute oven. If you don't have an electrical hook-up, we use it to make up to 8 slices of toast at a time. The BBQ is used in almost all meals. This item is considered essential.

f) Propane Stove. Most trailers have a hook-up for an outdoor propane stove. If you don't, you will need to get a stovetop one. Often you even find a second-hand one online.

The inside trailer stove is to be used for emergencies, such as it is freezing outside one morning and you want to boil water for coffee. Then you use the indoor stove to allow you to make the coffee without venturing into the arctic air and warm up the trailer so that you will get the courage to strip down and change into your clothes for the morning.

g) 1 to 20 Pound Converter Propane Adapter Hose. This item is directly related to items (d) and (e). If you have a tabletop stove or BBQ, you will need propane, of course. Those little bottles of propane can easily deplete a bank account, as they are $6 or more for each 1-pound container of propane.

But there is hope on the horizon. You can get an adapter at Walmart or a hardware store that converts the stove/BBQ connection from requiring to use only the tiny canisters to now be able to use the 20-pound tanks. It costs about $30, but it will pay for itself very quickly. This changes the price from six dollars or more per pound to about a dollar a pound, which is over an 80% discount on your propane costs.

Then you can just bring the 20-pound tank with you (or take the extra tank off your trailer if the trailer holds two and you are completely out), and hook it up, and voila! Propane at a fraction of the cost. We have found that a 20-pound tank can last us up to 5 weeks of daily use, even when we use it for multiple meals each day.

h) French Press Coffeemaker. If you don't have an electrical hook-up, a coffeemaker is not an option, and either way, it can be bulky.

We use a French press to make coffee. It takes up much less space, makes coffee under a minute after the water boils, and works under all conditions. It costs about $15 and is available in most kitchenware aisles. I have even found them at the Dollar Store for only a couple of bucks.

i) Dishwashing basins. After you make the mess, you have the joy of cleaning it up. Here, if you have full hookups, including sewer, you have the choice of bringing all the dirty dishes inside, washing, rinsing, and drying them, and then putting them back in their bins.

However, if you don't have unlimited sewer capacity or don't want the hassle of bringing dirty dishes inside the trailer, here is what we do.

We have two plastic tubs from the Dollar Store. They are made with thicker plastic, and sometimes they even say wash bins on their labels. You want ones that can handle heavyweight, as water is not light.

One of the bins is for washing the dishes, and the other is for rinsing. I prefer round ones to squares because they fit easier in my sink when filling.

The washing bins have multiple purposes. We use them during meal prep to bring out (and bring back in) the assortment of food and spices you need to take out of the cupboards and fridge. This works better than trying to fit it all in your arms and dropping the pickles all over your last pair of clean socks.

Even if we have full hookups, we still wash, rinse, and dry the dishes outside. We want the extra space outside to give enough room to the helpers. Plus, since all the dishes are stored in bins outside, it is easier to put them away.

One more thing… washing dishes with a lot of "stuff" on them is not fun on the best of days. It makes the dishwater turn very unpleasant in a hurry.

To address this, we wipe down the plates and bowls when there is a lot of mess (think spaghetti sauce, mustard, ketchup, salad dressing, BBQ sauce, etc.) with paper towels before putting the extra messy plates or bowls in the dishwater. We will either throw the dirty tissues in the garbage or use them to start the fire later that day.

j) Coolers. Extend Your Fridge Space. I bring an extra cooler for all beverages. We fill the cooler with a bag of ice each day, and it keeps everything cold and easily available without using valuable and very limited fridge space. This gives us several more cubic feet of useable space.

k) Sorting Food by Meals. It is easier to sort the foods in your trailer according to the most-used-for-meal type. For us, breakfast has more food variety than you would think. For example, we store bread, peanut butter, honey, oats, sugar, coffee in one plastic milk crate. It makes it easy just to need to grab the cream in the morning, throw it in the box with the rest of the breakfast items and take it outside. It is also easier when you are bringing it all back inside at the end of the meal.

l) If there is no room for an outdoor kitchen of any kind. You have to do the entire meal prep inside. If you have an electrical hook-up, I will use a crock-pot whenever possible. It allows you to do the majority of the meal prep in advance. It would also minimize the number of extra pots you have to clean. And you can heat the leftovers the next night.

Safety – What Precautions You Need to Take

There is a certain risk to living in a home on wheels. If somebody really wanted to, they could drive off with your home and everything you own. An RV door isn't exactly made of steel, and it wouldn't take much for somebody to smash it in if they really wanted to. However, dwelling on the risks isn't healthy. There are always risks in life.

Personal Safety

When You're Inside, Keep Your Doors and Windows Locked at All Times

Choose RV parks or parking spots that offer plenty of light. A gated park offers additional security.

Invest in a security light in your RV. This is basically the same thing you would put above your garage at home. The light shines when motion is detected to dissuade prospective intruders.

Avoid putting anything expensive outside or in the windows of your RV. You don't want to advertise what you have.

Consider having a dog travel with you. A barking dog is one of the best security systems on the planet.

Security cameras are an option if you are concerned. This allows you to see all the way around your RV while you are resting comfortably inside.

A security alarm is a good idea as well. If a window or door is opened, the alarm would sound. If you are in a park, other residents would be alerted.

Carrying a gun, taser or Mace is an option. If you do a lot of boondocking or camping in extremely rural areas, this may be a good thing.

Keep a cell phone charged and ready to go in case you need to call for help. Always know your location. A signal booster will assist you in receiving a signal in areas where reception is spotty.

RV Safety

It isn't always a bogeyman who can make your RV life unsafe. Your RV needs to be well-maintained to ensure your travels are safe. You also need to take steps to ensure the RV isn't a safety risk.

Turn off the propane stove before going on the move.

Install both a carbon monoxide and a smoke detector in your home.

Increase your following distance by 20 percent when you are driving an RV. A bigger rig takes longer to stop.

To avoid sheering the top of your RV, be aware of its height and pay attention to clearance signs.

Do not drive large Class A motor homes and some of the larger fifth wheels in high winds, especially on open roads. Pull over somewhere that provides a block from the wind.

Make sure your mirrors are adjusted to give you a good view of both lanes and behind you.

Check the tread on your tires regularly. A blown tire on an RV is much different from a car. Tires that are older than seven years should be replaced. Check that the tires are not underinflated. Use blocks and jacks to relieve tension on a single tire if you plan to stay in one place for longer than a few days.

Invest in roadside assistance that covers your RV.

Part VIII

–

RV Problems, Maintenance, and Travel Tips

Common RV Problems and Solutions

The best way to solve a problem quickly is to be prepared for it. The same applies to RV challenges that you may experience when you are on the road or camping.

Driving Into Overhead Obstructions

This problem is very common among new RV owners since some forget that an RV is much higher than an ordinary car. Driving an RV means you must learn to pay special attention to the possible risks from overhead obstructions.

Many new RV owners think they can rely on their eyesight to make a correct judgment of whether an obstruction will or will not cause a problem for the RV.

You can avoid being the latest victim of overhangs by measuring the height of your RV so that you know the minimum overhead clearance it needs. Add an extra foot to that minimum height just to be sure that your RV will be safe. Record this height and place it on a hard-to-miss location, such as on your dashboard, so that you can compare the height notice on overhead objects with what you have recorded as the clearance you need. When in doubt, err on the side of caution by avoiding passing under that low-hanging obstruction instead of risking severe damage to your RV.

Tire Blowouts

A blown tire can be extremely dangerous for you and other road users, so you should do everything possible to avoid this problem. Maintain a spare tire on hand at all times. Check all tires for visible signs of wear or damage and ensure that they are all inflated to the recommended level (such as cracks on the sidewall). If a tire blows out while you are driving, be very cautious as you steer the RV off the road. Once you have removed the RV from the road, ask all occupants to exit it, then follow the tire replacement instructions in the RV manual.

You can call for roadside assistance if you feel that you cannot change the blown tire safely on your own.

Battery Failure

Battery failure can cause the lights in your RV to go out or the appliances inside to stop working. Check the fluid level in your RV battery on a regular basis to avoid this problem. You should (at least) conduct this check before you embark on a trip.

Top up the distilled water to the recommended level and clean the battery terminals so that dirt and rust do not cause it to discharge. You can also install cut-off switches to avoid power loss while appliances are switched off. Investing in a dry battery may save you from constantly worrying about fluid levels in your RV battery.

If the battery eventually fails, check the fluid level before you plug it into the AC outlet to charge it. If this problem keeps occurring, consider that your battery is worn out and buy a replacement battery.

In the event that you are traveling and your battery fails because of corrosion, an interestingly effective tip for you is to pour Mountain Dew (yes, the soda) on the corrosion. This should melt the corrosion away and allow you to start your vehicle

Toilet Issues

Nothing can be as troubling to a first-time RV owner as an RV toilet that has malfunctioned. This problem can cause toilet smells to circulate the entire RV or render the toilet unusable for days until the problem is fixed. You can avoid RV toilet issues by using toilet paper that is recommended for RVs (the variety that quickly breaks down). It would really help if you also emptied the tank as soon as it fills up (there is a sensor in the tank to alert you of this). Avoid toilet seal malfunctions by keeping the seal well lubricated so that it remains pliant.

Remove the toilet and replace the slide valve gasket if you notice that water no longer stays in the toilet bowl. The RV manual has instructions that you can follow to perform this task on your own. If water keeps running in your toilet, then that is a sign that the valve is not closing completely. If this is the case, you also need to replace that valve in the same way as you did for the valve that keeps water in the bowl.

Prevention has always been better than reacting after a problem has occurred, so you should invest every effort necessary so that you learn how to avoid the problems above.

RV Maintenance

Deal with your RV, and it will deal with you. An upbeat RV will take all of you over the nation for some miles, permitting you brilliant open doors for experience and memory-making.

Keeping up an RV should be possible DIY, or you can take it into the carport or administration stations to be kept up. It relies upon your jack of all trades capacities and inclinations and, in addition, the progression of what should be kept up.

In this part, we will take a gander at what DIY support and checks you can do intermittently during the time that is certain to lessen costs. I will give a fast specify to dumping since this is an unavoidable piece of RV living.

DIY and Preventative Support

The following are a couple of things you can do yourself to keep your RV in great condition:

- Voltage – Using an electronic multi-meter, monitor the voltage of your RV and AC. Take after your RV manual for the right voltage when your RV is not charging.
- Caulking – Frequently check the caulking around your RV. Water harm is your RV's foe. Evacuate any old caulking and supplant it with new caulking.

It might be tedious; in any case, it is justified regardless of the yield. Pay special mind to any splits and openings; repair if necessary.

- Is everything secure? – Regularly watch that your RV's nuts, fasteners, and screws are tight. Commit significantly more thoughtfulness regarding the outside of your RV than the inside. A screwdriver and torque will keep your RV secure.
- Lube – Regularly watch that pivots, rails, and bolts are all around greased up.
- Wax your RV – Make beyond any doubt that your RV has UV insurance by waxing it with a decent quality wax. Before re-waxing your RV, give it a decent scour.
- Tires – Use your RV manual as a manual for suggested tire weight. Guarantee that your tires are at the right weight before every excursion.

Mull over where you are setting out to and the effect it will have on your tire weight. You might need to alter your tire weight as indicated by climate as well.

Ensure that your tire fasteners are fixed before voyaging. Watch tire string and check for any breaks or punctures.

- Lights – Carry safety lights for your RV both inside and outside. Ensure that your RV outside lights and signal lights are functioning admirably. Keep combines close by on the off chance that you have to change a wire before voyaging.
- Under the RV – Occasionally review underneath your RV. Pay special mind to erosion, free links, or some other broken things. Repair as required or take your RV to the carport for some expert help.
- Sensors – Check that your carbon monoxide, propane, and smoke sensors are working. Change batteries if necessary.

Standard Adjusting and Upkeep

With your RV being a home on wheels as an auto, it will require general administrations and upkeep. These standard adjusting and upkeep include:

- Oil and channel changes – your RV should have its oil and channels changed around 3,000 to 4,000 miles. On the off chance that you are pulling a troop or RV trailer, your truck will require its general oil and channel changes.

Channel changes incorporate fuel, coolant, air, and water-driven.

- Generator support – your generator will require its oil and channels changed intermittently as well. On the off chance that you are staying at an RV stop or campground for a noteworthy timeframe, run your generator once every month to keep it in great condition. Take after your upkeep guides for more particular subtle elements.
- Brake check – Keep your brakes working admirably to guarantee your well-being and that of your family's. The exact opposite thing you'd need is to experience brake disappointment.
- Rooftop investigation and upkeep – If your RV has an elastic rooftop, organize it to be dealt with yearly (least). Like clockwork, have your rooftop professionally reviewed.

Whatever upkeep or administrations your RV requires, take after your RV support manual to correct subtle elements on when to benefit your RV and what to pay special attention to.

A Snappy Word on Dumping

Docking at a dump station to dump your waste tanks is the less spectacular side of RV living, yet an important errand in any case. Your RV accompanies three tanks, a water tank, a dark tank, and a dark tank.

These tanks should be kept perfect and all around kept up. This incorporates dumping the waste and cleaning the tanks. In the event that your tanks are not kept clean, you won't have a precise pointer of how full your waste tanks are. In a perfect world, you need to dump your tanks when they are either totally full or 75% full.

The cardinal administers of dumping is never dumped on the ground. Continuously spotless your tanks at a dumping station or utilize the full hookup at your RV stop (that is, whether they have a full hookup).

Here are a couple of tips and traps to make the dumping knowledge a bit smoother:

Put resources into another hose – The hose that accompanies your RV is not going to be exceptionally dependable. In addition to it, it doesn't attend an augmentation or other essential connectors. A sewer pack ought to carry out the employment. Here is a rundown of other hardware you should dump your tanks:

A clear hose elbow with the goal that you can see what is going on. Purchase the point of the elbow most appropriate to your requirements.

- A committed 50-foot water hose. This hose can be a garden hose and ought to just be utilized for dumping.
- Disposable latex gloves.
- Hose support to give your hose a descending slant and keep it off the ground.
- A hose augmentation just on the off chance that you require additional length on your hose. Maybe be sheltered than too bad.
- Sewer chemicals – Since most septic tanks can be harmed by formaldehyde, so attempt to abstain from utilizing chemicals with this substance as a part of it. Utilize sewer chemicals with alert.
- Disinfectant chemicals.

Dumping your tanks – To dump your tanks, ensure that you are wearing your gloves. Interface the sewer hose, ensuring that the association is tight. To watch that there are no holes in your association, open your dim tank somewhat.

When you have set up that your association is secure, open up your dark tank. Exhaust your dark tank totally. Continue to your particular sewer hose to the dark tank flush. Turn on the water and clean your tank until get water runs out.

To clean within the dark water tank, turn the dark handle in so that the water flushes into the tank for around three minutes. Revive the handle, so the water flushes out. Rehash this procedure until the water coming up short on the tank is spotless. Kill the water and push the dark handle in.

How about we proceed onward to the dark tank. The dim tank is flushed after the dark tank in order to utilize the water to flush any build-up operating at a profit tank. The procedure is the same as the dark tank.

When you have wrapped up your tanks, evacuate the hose and top the sewer connector to keep any drippings.

Your dark tank ought to get a catalyst after each dump and your dim tank after each fourth dump. Flush all your hardware and splash with disinfectant, including the handles, the sewer line, et cetera.

Since you comprehend what to search for with respect to support and how to dump your tanks, you are prepared for life out and about.

What to Know and Where to Go

Choosing a Destination

RVParky: This app is an RV park directory written by an RVer with user-generated reviews, images, and information. It works with GPS and displays RV parks, campgrounds, and RV-friendly stores on a clickable map, and it works equally well on mobile devices or computers.

Free Camping: This is an RV community-driven app and website that helps you find user-reviewed free camping sites of all types on a clickable map, then uses its built-in trip planner to map your trip. You can also filter results by amenities desired. It is free; however, you will need to create an account to get the most benefit from it.

Reserve America: Reserve America is a free membership-based app and website. It is unique in that you can search for, find, and reserve a spot within the app, including hiking trips, day-use facilities, lodging, and other outdoor activities like fishing trips. It is one-stop shopping.

RVLife: A subscription mobile device app that helps you find a campground, fine-tune it with multiple levels of clickable amenities, read the reviews, and map the trip from within the app. A unique attribute of this app is the downloadable map for when you are out of the range of cell towers.

Recreation.gov: Federal facility directory website and app that draws from 12 federal agencies such as the National Forest Service, National Park Service, and Bureau of Land Management. This resource also has a trip builder that helps you search for a site across 3,500 federal facilities.

How to Get There

RV Trip Wizard: Find campgrounds, points of interest, determine the cost, and set driving times and distances with this web-based application. This application is different in several ways from other trip planners. First, Whereas RV trip planners tend to show only the campgrounds affiliated with their respective publishers, RVTW shows all campgrounds. Second, it uses a map interface to set driving time and distance via concentric user-determined circles. You determine how large the circles are based upon your endurance. Third, it has cost monitoring features built-in that allows you to factor in tolls, fuel, campgrounds, food, and other costs to watch the overall trip cost.

Copilot: This is a highly recommended, version-specific navigation and traffic app for cars, trucks, or RVs that requires an annual $29.95 membership. The app looks like a conventional GPS unit and allows for out-of-cell tower use via downloadable offline maps that work with the GPS chip in your device.

While You Are Traveling

GPS Units

Many RVers prefer to use a separate GPS device for their travels. There are many from which to use, and RVers tend to choose the RV-specific units that provide the live-traffic capability. The benefit of using stand-alone GPS units is they usually have much larger screens that are not obscured by sunlight, they do not tie up your smart device, nor are they dependent upon either cell tower service or downloadable maps that can clog up your device. Expect to pay upwards of $300 for premium units, such as the Garmin RV 770 LMT-S or the Rand McNally RVND 7730 LM.

Map

The Rand McNally Motor Carrier's Atlas is the RVers best off-line friend. It is the same atlas commercial trucker drivers use, and it is extremely helpful in showing roads with weight, height, axle, and length limitations. Expect to pay around $20 for this atlas in softcover format or around $75 for laminated, spiral-bound versions. The benefit of using this is to "sanity-check" your GPS, to see the entire route at once, to enable less stressful on-the-fly travel planning.

iExit

This is a free, web-based and mobile device application that watches your location on the highway and displays upcoming gas, food, shelter, and rest stops by highway exit number. When you click on an exit, the app lists its services, including the price of fuel. It connects to other apps such as Yelp and Google Maps, so you can click to review or click to get directions. You can either discover and map the stops ahead of time or find yourself on the map via your mobile device's location services. If you are going to keep an app going while on the road, this is the one.

Rest Stops

This app enables you to find a rest stop by drilling down by state, highway, and direction of travel. Once found, you can get directions with Waze, Google Maps, or Apple Maps from within the app. The app also shows RV dump stations.

Sidebar

Temporary/overnight stops.

Big Box Overnighting

Call ahead, introduce yourself to the manager if you can, buy something while you are there, do not run your generator or kick out your slides, pick up after yourself, and park out of the way. Walmart, Costco, Sam's, Cabela's, Camping World, Cracker Barrel, and truck stops are the most common stops.

Making Money on the Road

We have touched on the options of working for a living while on the road. Have a quick look, if you haven't already done so, at our essential tips. In this, we will go into more detail about the ways you can fund your RV lifestyle. Finding suitable employment can be an important element for many RVers. Especially if you do not have the means to "up sticks" and travel around the country or even the world. It is possible and practical to work while you travel. This can be a major source of funding that will enable you to live the RV lifestyle, both long and short-term. Life on the road does not have to be as expensive as traditional living within a fixed base. Most people still need to earn a living to pay for the basics and the odd luxury. Regardless of your personal circumstances, even if you're retired or not in the best of health, you can still earn a living whilst on the road. There are so many different options available. There is something out there that will suit everyone.

Seasonal Employment

There are seasonal jobs all around the world and all year round.

Working on farms picking crops, such as fruit and vegetables. This type of work is best for those who are fit and active, as it can be quite labor-intensive. It usually involves lots of bending down, dependent on the crop. It will provide a temporary income. You may even get to eat the crops that you're picking. Whilst hard work is a prerequisite; it should also be satisfying, as you will be working outdoors. Being close to nature can give you a new lease on life, especially if most of your employment has been city-based and indoors. This type of work is often found in local advertisements. It might be worth asking the camp host if they are aware of any local crop growers looking for field workers for their harvest. There are also online job sites that include seasonal work in their listings.

Not all seasonal work is crop gathering this is just one option for harvest time.

You could consider applying for work on the Mesa Verde, which is a national park. There are many campgrounds within this designated UNESCO World Heritage Site. These jobs are often tourism-related:

- **Retail** - Sales, shelf filing, serving, cleaning.
- **Catering** - Sales, cooking, waitering, bar work, cleaning.
- **Sports-related** - Activities assistant, pool staff, lifeguards, instructors, campsite workers putting tents up, crèche work, horse work, bike work, golf, fishing, skiing, water sports, cleaners.
- **Hotelier work** - Maintenance, housekeeping, room or maid services, reception, security.
- **Driving** - Minibuses, tours, taxis in local towns.
- **Language facilitator** - Translators (if you have more than one language).

There is a vast variety of seasonal jobs, especially near the coast or mountains. It's worth pointing out that those who can work the whole season, usually from April to October, are often preferred to those who want shorter-term contracts.

To start your search for this type of employment, try the online website www.coolworks.com. You can apply well ahead of time and set up work in different places. This way you can still keep on the move, working in different areas as you travel. Some seasonal positions come with a parking space for your RV, often situated in the country's most picturesque areas. If money is not so essential for you, then you could consider volunteer work. This is a great way to get to know the locals and to be able to contribute to the communities that you are visiting.

If you are considering working overseas, don't forget to check out if you need a work visa or permit. Do your research and find out about all the legal paraphernalia that might go with such a commitment.

Camp Site Work: Also Known as "Workamping"

This involves working for a number of hours a week, usually around 10–20, at the campground where you are staying. In return, you may get free camping fees and hook up. Sometimes the employer will pay the minimum wage as well, for whichever state you are in. This type of work can vary and include jobs such as maintenance, site hosts - greeting new arrivals, allocating pitches, taking ground rent, site shops, general cleaning, grass cutting, gardening tasks, and landscaping skills. If you like meeting people and getting involved in the site that you're staying at, then this can be a great way of life. Finding this type of work is fairly straightforward. You could ask around at different sites when you arrive and stay a while longer once you find work. If you want a more organized approach, there are many websites to search on, such as www.work-for-rvers-and-campers.com, www.snowbirdrvtrails.com, and www.camphost.org. They deal with employment at campgrounds all around the US. It is possible to find seasonal work all year round, but you will need to go to the winter sport villages during the colder months. Skiing villages will be busy and wanting temporary staff. For employment in the winter months, you can try resorts in Colorado, such as Aspen, Beaver Creek, and Breckenridge, to name but a few.

If you've never done anything like this before, then a quick web search will bring up various sites where RVers, just like you, are discussing their working life. They are happy to share their experiences and let you know of the good and bad points of working on the road. As you become more experienced with each year, you could find yourself applying for the team leaders, management, and supervisory posts. It is all there for the picking from national parks, resorts, ranches, and farms, to campgrounds, skiing villages, and water-based entertainment. There are an abundance of temporary jobs where you can gain experience and have fun all at the same time

Artisan Items

Turn your crafting hobbies and handmade goods into a lucrative business. With the added bonus of being an RV owner, you can travel the country, attending craft fairs and markets to sell your wares. The beauty of this type of work is that the possibilities are endless. Almost everyone can turn their hand to some craft or other, whether it be:

Making Costume Jewelry

- **Hand Made Greetings Cards.** For all occasions, all year round. People will pay that little bit extra to have individual and unique handmade items.
- **Knitting or crochet.** If you have either of these skills, you can offer an array of goods, such as clothing, dolls, computer sleeves, covers for digital readers, or phones. The list is endless. If you've never knitted before, then give it a go. It is one of those relaxing and productive pastimes for males and females alike. Plus, it might just earn you a living.
- **Woodwork.** Turn your hand to making toys or furniture and gifts. If you are a skilled carpenter already, then you may find work, such as maintaining premises. You might even offer your services to fix or improve the furniture in your fellow RVers' vehicles.
- **Photography or artwork.** Sell your prints or pop them in frames. With the explosion of digital cameras and cell phones, it seems everyone can be the next Ansel Adams or Annie Leibovitz. While visiting stunning locations, you could photograph or paint the scenery and then sell them to tourists.

Tapestries or cross-stitching can be stunning once complete, and if done well, will sell on.

Creating decorative items is an ideal activity for an RV lifestyle. The goods you make should be relatively small and light, making them easy to store. You could do your work in the dinette area or sit out in the sunshine with a panoramic view.

Using Your Own Set Skills

Utilize any other skills that you already have, such as hairdressing, DIY, gardening, mechanics, or even cleaning. These are all skills that others may be happy to pay for or even barter. You cut your fellow travelers' hair whilst they fix your chair, so to speak.

Once you land at your campground, try putting a small ad in a local shop window to let your new neighbors know about your services. Take photographs of your successes and build up a portfolio to show future customers. It's up to you to prove how trustworthy and reliable you are because locals may be wary of travelers. A friendly and open disposition will go a long way to earning their trust.

You could also consider studying while on the move, as there are many online courses whereby you never need to attend a classroom. You could use your studies to improve your employment prospects. It's a good message for future employers. Informing them that, whilst you might live your life a little different from the norm, you still care about being competitive in the working market. Plus, studying at your leisure means that you may well enjoy it. It's not quite the same as being at school where you had to do it. You are doing it for you and no one else.

Working Online

With the explosion in the ownership of smart cell phones and tablets and wide cell network coverage, it has never been easier to get online. Even while you are on the move. The ability to connect to the web wherever you are means that online working is a real option for those who live the RV lifestyle. Yet another great way of earning an income to fund your travels. You are not just confined to using your cells or tablets either. Many campgrounds have internet access, sometimes for a small fee, but often for free. Many public areas now give free internet access, particularly cafes, bars, and restaurants. So, there is a plethora of options to get online and earn some money. You may be able to keep your current job by telecommuting, as it is often called. This is a popular and growing choice for many professionals. You can communicate with your employer by using applications (apps), such as Skype or Facetime. It is a great way to keep in touch with the boss while you continue your travels.

Online Auction Sites

Online auction sites are a great way to earn extra cash and can also be fun to run. The most popular one, eBay, has been going for over 20 years, and selling on there has never been simpler:

Register for an eBay account at no cost whatsoever. Begin by creating private listings. Once you build up your stock, change to a business account with a store at a later date.

Register for a PayPal account, also at no cost. PayPal runs like an online banking system and enables you to receive payments or buy things yourself. PayPal is growing ever popular with many online shops and is useful when you are traveling. It can link up with your personal bank account, making it simple to transfer money.

Quick and easy - both of the above can be set up in a matter of minutes. Once you have an eBay and PayPal account, you can start selling to the recently estimated 160 million eBay members worldwide. Don't just stick to selling to customers in your own country. Be confident and sell your wares overseas. All you need is access to a post office or other couriers such as FedEx.

Part IX

—

RV Life Hacks: Staying Connected, and FAQs

Staying Connected

Adventure-hungry wanderers have always existed, but in the past, they have often been marginalized or viewed as outsiders for their unconventional choice not to settle down at a permanent address. Stereotypes associated with nomads have historically ranged from mocking to downright demeaning.

The Desert Fathers of the early Christian church were social outcasts who chose a celibate, minimalist life steeped in prayer and contemplation in the great unknown. The hippies of the 1960s who lived out of their vans, preaching love and peace, were a laughingstock of their parents' generation. The first modern American homeschoolers in the 1980s created widespread controversy in certain states.

Millennials Have It Made

The good news is that in the current decade, people are generally less inclined to question you. Though there will always be those who judge your decision not to participate in the rat race, there is an increasing number of people who are sympathetic, if not entirely supportive, of your decision to be a full-time RV traveler. And the rest? Well, they might secretly long for what you've chosen, too, but they will resist out of fear.

It isn't a secret to anyone that millennials haven't exactly inherited the best financial situation. Time Magazine reports that while most young people dream of owning homes, they find the possibility deeply unlikely. A combination of extreme disillusionment with the economy and a sense of hopelessness—a feeling that no amount of hard work will ever amount to anything—has driven many young individuals and families to reconsider their priorities.

For many, this has meant resigning themselves to being lifelong renters. It is admirable that millennials are putting in long hours even with little promise of upward mobility. But for others (including yourself, if you've read this far), the downfall of the American Dream is just too disappointing of a reality to face. Long-term RVers are giving up their ideals of homeownership in favor of something that sounds more financially doable and provides more opportunity for excitement and fulfillment: a life on the road.

There was a time when selling your house, dropping everything, and trading the commuter line for the rugged terrain meant certain things in regards to your social life. It was expected that you would lose touch with friends and family due to the distance as well as the uncertainty about the next time you'd roll into a gas station with a payphone. Up until the 1990s, you were lucky if you could send regular postcards to your family back home. However, the Internet has altered everything so drastically that the modern nomad's life is nothing like that of those who came before us.

They paved the way and made the thrill and unpredictable nature of road life seem cool and appealing. But the simple fact is that we are living in a different era than they were. Today's RVers often choose out of frustration with the fast-paced digital time period we live in. But in a strangely comforting paradox, many are also filled with gratitude for the fact that they are lucky enough to remain connected to their loved ones.

DIY Photojournalism

Take a quick glance at Instagram, and you will see more than a few highly popular accounts run by individuals and couples alike. The photos are bright, slick, and professional. The fashion is impeccable. The RVs are in beautiful condition. But the landscape? That hasn't changed a bit. It's still majestic. It still takes your breath away to witness it, even through a photograph. The lay of the land hasn't changed, only the way we perceive it and interact with it.

Whether you're swilling scotch in a dive bar in rural Nevada, camping in the Everglades, or gambling in Dawson City, you can share photos and commentary on your experience with the press of a button. Not only that, but if you use social media effectively, you can monetize your adventures by blogging about them and inspire complete strangers to make similar life choices.

If you're a good writer, photographer, or both, you can create your own photo essays and share them with millions of people. There was a time when you needed to be in New York, London, Paris, or LA to reach so many people at once, but now, all you need is a relatively new smartphone and a Wi-Fi hotspot.

It isn't hard to find those, either. Even in rural areas, you can remain connected to the Internet, and many campgrounds provide access for a small fee. Maintaining your Facebook account while on the road allows you to stay updated on what your family is up to. FaceTime with family members is simple if you have an iPhone. If you're concerned that your kids will miss out on precious time with Grandma and Grandpa, they can have face-to-face interaction from thousands of miles away. That is the age we are in, and it is a wonderful thing.

Of course, no matter how meaningful it may be, communicating online is still no match for real, human connections. It is important to keep your kids—and yourself—involved in social communities and meet new people no matter what town or city you visit. Interact with people from various backgrounds and walks of life. Get to know your campground "neighbors," even if you're only setting up shop for a few nights. Sit with them beneath the stars, share a meal with them, and learn their stories. Then, when you leave, add them on Facebook or Instagram and promise to keep in touch.

The most fascinating thing about the social media age is how it allows people from all over the world to stay connected even after only one meeting. How many of us have heard our parents or grandparents wistfully recall a chance encounter with a friendly couple on vacation, which they never saw again because they didn't get their address or phone number? This isn't a dilemma that millennials can relate to. If anything, social media has made it almost too easy to track down that nice person you met at the campground after you leave.

Some RVers truly wish to be liberated and free of all attachments to modern society. The minimalist movement is growing at exponential rates for this very reason. But one of the most common reasons that even the savviest RVers stay on social media? They have friends in every corner of the world.

Sure, there is an element of narcissism involved in showing pictures of your exciting life on the road. But for most people who choose to stay "plugged in" despite living out of a small camper van in the woods, the motivation is clear: they want to know they have friends they can reach out to anywhere.

Once you have even one foreign friend, six degrees of separation starts to work its magic, and suddenly, you are linked to many more people than you could ever imagine. If traveling abroad someday is one of your ultimate goals, this is an incredible benefit to staying connected to social media. Even if you only keep one account up and running, it reminds people that you're still there within reach and gives them a quick and easy way to reach out to you if they happen to be in your neck of the woods.

Most people have a "dream vacation" in mind. Even if you've never spent a long time contemplating the possibility of where you would go because it seems unrealistic, there's a good chance that you could drum up the name of one particular place that sounds especially enticing to you. Maybe you've always longed to see the Coral Reef, build a school in Uganda, sip merlot in the French countryside, or ski in Colorado. Maybe the Norwegian culture fascinates you, or you'd love to visit a pub in the Scottish Highlands.

Whatever the case may be, if you open yourself to unconventional possibilities, you might find yourself a whole lot closer to achieving your seemingly impossible dream. At campgrounds all across the world, nomadic, ambitious, and fearless travelers just like yourself are dreaming similar dreams.

The world may have seven billion people, but the more you see of it, the smaller it becomes. So you could start at a campground a few miles from home and meet someone who knows someone who has a housesitting opportunity in the Swiss Alps or the Upper West Side.

Without social media, you might have to go through a longer chain of connections before you ever reach those people and let them know you're interested in their offer. All you have to do with social media is send them a quick email or register on Airbnb to prove you're a real person. Making connections worldwide is really that easy, and the more people you meet, the more people will be able to vouch for your trustworthy nature. Before you know it, you could be taking your travels a lot further than you could ever have imagined.

In 2017 and beyond, the call of the wild does not mean sacrificing your connection to the real world. It offers the best of both worlds. We have so much power in our handheld devices and the ability to use them to influence and inspire others. Why not use it to the best of our ability?

Domicile, Mail, Voting, Banking, and Taxes

Choosing Your State of Domicile

The most essential decisions you'll make when picking up your roots and living a mobile lifestyle is deciding which state you'll call home. You'll often hear RVers joke that "home is where you park it" or "home is where you hook up," and even though you may consider yourself a full-time traveling nomad, for legal purposes, you will still need to claim a physical location as "home." Many businesses, and of course, the government, will require you to have a legal, physical address for things like your driver's license, taxes, and bank accounts, to name a few.

RV Terms to Know

Domicile

According to Black's Law Dictionary, "a person's domicile is the place where he lives or has his home. In a strict and legal sense, that is properly the domicile of a person where he has his true, fixed, permanent home and principal establishment, and to which he intends to return whenever he is absent." Simply put, for RVers, it is the place (state, city, address) you choose as your home, especially for legal and tax purposes, have a substantial connection with and intend to make a fixed and permanent home.

Residence

This is where you reside, usually your home. It means living in a particular locality and simply requires bodily presence as an inhabitant in a given place. You can live in more than one place, but only one of them can be designated as your domicile.

You may not have heard the term domicile before, as it's not something people usually talk about in their regular lives. For most people, their primary home or residence is also their domicile, as they are usually the same. But for people who have more than one home in different parts of the country or world, choosing the one as their primary residence will be considered their domicile. As an RVer, your home is traveling with you. In the winter, it might be by the beach in Florida, and in the summer, it might be situated among the mountains in Colorado. So, where do you truly live?

Domicile is defined as where you consider home to be or plan to return to after your travels. A residence is where you live temporarily. You can have as many residences as you want, but only one domicile. You might hit the road with the intention of finding a new place to call home and put down roots again. However, while you're figuring that out, you'll still need to declare one location as your domicile.

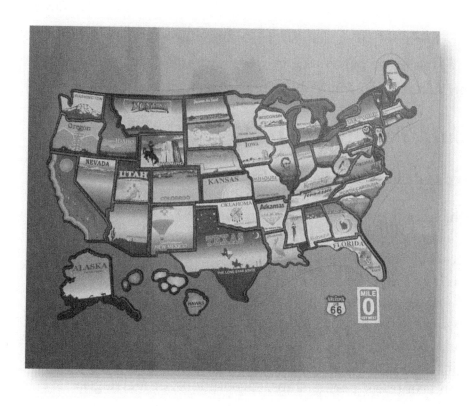

Factors to Think About

You might choose to continue to claim the city and state you departed from as your domicile. Perhaps you have family or friends in the region who are fine with you using their address as your own for an extended period of time as if you are staying in a spare room or sleeping on their couch. Assume that you are looking for a more permanent residence solution. In that case, this can be a much more complicated question, as there are many factors to consider when choosing your optimal domicile. Domicile is a highly personal choice, and only you will know enough about your situation to know what is right for you. Detailed analysis of each variable is beyond the scope of this book, let alone this, and we are not legal experts on the important subject of domicile, but the information we share in this will help guide your thinking and let you know where you need to do more research, allowing you to make an informed and confident decision. You may also choose to get legal advice to assist you in this matter.

If you are looking to make a change, Florida, South Dakota, and Texas are all good places for you to start your research, as these states are RVer-friendly, making it easier to handle many things (like vehicle registration) for those of us living a mobile life. The other advantage of setting up your new "home" in an RV-friendly state is that with so many other RVers also claiming it as home, the RVers and organizations become very influential when it comes to local laws. In some areas, there are more RVers registered as voters than there are people who physically reside there. Escapees RV Club, in particular, is very strong in providing advocacy for RVers, as they have so many members, a significant percentage of whom are full-time RVers, which makes for a very large "population" in the town where they are headquartered.

Where Should Your Domicile Be?

Here is a list of considerations that might affect your domicile choice:

- The length of time you plan on RVing.
- Whether or not you plan to sell your traditional home.
- The location of your employer or place of business.
- Tax laws relating to real estate, pensions, sales, income, wills, estates, investments, etc.
- Health insurance availability and pricing.
- Vehicle insurance, inspection, and registration requirements.
- Voting and jury duty eligibility.
- Community involvement and/or political environment.
- Laws around contracts, partnerships, corporations, or marriages.
- Laws related to possessions, permitting, and medical treatments.
- Education tuition for you or your children.
- Licensing requirements for large vehicles.
- Ease of working with a state or local government when out of state.
- Weather conditions during the time of year when you might need to visit.
- The total time you plan to spend in a state or county per year.
- How many family members and friends live there?
- Your interest in returning to the area when not traveling.

Of course, the simpler your life is before your transition to RV life, the easier the decisions are. The amount of research required is directly related to how many of the earlier listed variables affect you, and doing your research can allow you to maximize the benefits for your individual circumstances. This will explain some of these topics in greater detail to give you more perspective on their impact, starting with taxes.

Taxes: Sales, Income, and Property

Every government needs to generate revenue one way or another. Some states focus on doing that through property tax or income tax, while others might focus on sales tax. If you are looking to purchase a $300,000 motorhome, you might be drawn to a state that charges no sales tax when others charge over 8%. That alone could mean a savings of $24,000 in sales tax. On the other hand, if you plan to spend only $30,000 on your RV, and your income is $100,000 per year, you might be more interested in a state that has lower income tax versus sales tax. California has income tax rates as high as 13%, while Texas, Florida, South Dakota, Nevada, Washington, Wyoming, and Alaska have no state income tax.

Perhaps you are approaching or are already at retirement age and have income from social security, investments, dividends, rental properties, or a military or other pension. Maybe you have a large nest egg that you plan to leave to your children and are mindful of inheritance taxes. Tax rules and rates will vary for all of those different revenue streams depending on your chosen domicile, so this decision can get pretty complicated.

Property-related taxes can be important too. If you don't own property, you don't have to pay property tax; however, if you DO own property in a state with a high property tax, your RV loan payment may end up being less than what you used to pay in property tax alone. If you currently own property and are planning on selling that property to venture into full-time RV life, be very careful about changing your domicile before you sell and close on that property. Some states—Maryland and Rhode Island are two examples—currently have a property-related tax that very few know about, including some realtors. This special tax comes into effect only if you are selling a property and are not currently domiciled in that same state. The tax in Maryland is 7.5% of the total transaction price, so if you sold a $400,000 home, you could get hit with a $30,000 bill that you could have avoided by simply keeping your driver's license and domicile in Maryland until after the sale of your property closed. Sometimes it makes sense to change your domicile before you hit the road but not always, so do your research.

Other Factors: Insurance, Education, Ease, and Ethics

Once you figure out which state has the most favorable tax environment for you, look at other important factors that may sway your decision about domicile, even though their financial impact may be lower.

Insurance

Insurance is a big factor as, similar to taxes; there are several types of insurance. We have known several RVers who changed their state of domicile solely based on health insurance needs. Many states do not support national insurance coverage, which can be a deal-breaker for some full-time RVers who travel all around the country. The rules and regulations around health insurance continue to change often and fast, so again, this is something you'll need to keep a regular eye on in case things change in a way that affects you.

Vehicle insurance rates vary across the country, and if you have a poor driving record or a history of insurance claims, this can result in large swings in the cost of insuring your RV. Insurance rates are based on historical data and can change at any time, but at the time of writing, Ohio had the lowest, and Florida had the highest vehicle insurance rates. The rates in Florida can be as much as four times higher than those in Ohio. This may not be enough to outweigh other considerations, but it is definitely a factor to consider in the big picture.

Winterizing and De-Winterizing Your RV

During the winter, your trailer is helpless against costly harm from bursting channels, broken water stockpiling, snow gathering, and that's just the beginning. So it's pivotal to winterize as soon your season closes. If you have to live in a colder atmosphere, you have to winterize your RV no later than the fall because winterizing your RV is cheap, but repairing is not.

Winterizing

It is far much more comfortable and more straightforward than you think. You need to follow these steps:

Step 1

Deplete the water tank by expelling the deplete cap located on the underbelly of your trailer.

Step 2

Release pressure from the water warmer and remove the drain plug. The deplete attachment may likewise be the anode rod. Be alert when soothing weight, as the water might be hot if the water warmer has been operational. (Rural Water Heaters have an anode rod with a 1/16 nut. Atwood Water Heaters have no anode bar. They utilize plastic, so they don't harm the aluminum tank they are strung into. It requires a 7/8 socket attachment.)

Step 3

Turn the water heater bypass valve from the inline position.

Step 4

Turn the valve at the water pump from the inline position to the sidestep position.

Step 5

Find the water passage on the outside of the unit. Associate the hose to the water passage, and after that, plunge the tube into a holder of a liquid antifreeze agent.

Step 6

Turn on the water pump. It will begin pumping radiator fluid through your RV's water framework. Starting at the water spigot nearest to the pump, open each hot tap until the point that radiator fluid turns out and at that point, close the valve (single lever faucets must be done on both hot and cold).

Step 7

In the end, make sure to winterize your RV's water segment. It is frequently the most overlooked step. Turn the water pump off and open the water spigot to assuage pressure from the water framework. Next, expel the screen from the city water segment and depress the spring-stacked check valve tenderly until the point that radiator fluid discharges the rest of the water from the water segment line.

De-Winterizing

Deciding when to de-winterize your RV relies upon the atmosphere where you live. A few states warm up sooner than others.

Ordinarily, mid-April is a safe time to de-winterize your RV anyplace in the United States.

It is done by following these steps:

Step 1

Open and deplete your water tank.

Deplete is commonly situated on the underbelly of your RV close to the stairs.

Step 2

Close the drain, connect a new water hose to your RV's water tank and fill up your water tank.

Step 3

Locate the power pump and utilize a power drill with a square head to evacuate the board and gain admittance to your water pump.

Step 4

At the water pump, find the winterize hose. Flip the valve on the tube so the water pump will pull from the new water tank and turn on the water pump.

Step 5

Open every one of the taps in your RV (hot and cold) to permit the radiator fluid in your framework to flush out.

Faucets incorporate kitchen sink, shower, can, restroom sink, and so on. Close all the taps once you see water coming out of them.

Step 6

Shut off the water pump and Open your kitchen sink taps again and keep them on to permit any following measures of antifreeze to exit.

Step 7

Go to one of your sinks and turn on the hot side of the spigot. Hold up a couple of minutes to build up the pressure. Once the water has built up a suitable strength, then you are good to go.

Gadgets

Your RV is your new home, and you want to make RV-living as easy as possible. The simplest way is to purchase gadgets. Unlike with a typical house, the gadgets you need in your RV should be lightweight and space-efficient.

To help you select the best gadgets for your RV-living, here are some fantastic items you should check out:

Air Lounger

There are many benefits of having an air lounger in your RV. These products are easy to use since you don't need to tire yourself out using an air pump. You can inflate your air lounger with ease by holding it in the wind.

The durable material used in designing air loungers makes them suitable for various outdoor conditions, such as damp grass and rocky or rough campsites, depending on where you park your RV. They are lightweight and collapse to a compact size that makes them easy to store. Air loungers also sell at an affordable price, making it possible to get one, even on a budget.

Folding Bikes

These offer lots of functionality to you as an RV-living gadget. Being foldable, the bike storage is much easier, considering you have limited space in your RV. You can also select a suitable bike for the terrain you will be camping in more frequently.

When camping, there are times when you will want to explore or hike. Having a folding bike in your RV will offer the mobility you need to make your exploration a lot easier.

There are different factors to consider when selecting your folding bike, such as:

- Wheel size.
- Weight.
- Folding mechanism.
- Frame material.

- Electric option.

Evaluating each product you find attractive using the criteria listed above will help you select a product that meets your needs and preferences.

Smart Space Heaters

When living in your RV, you need to prepare for the winter season. It is best to prepare beforehand to ensure you have enough time to get things in place. One of the best means of supplemental heat for your RV is a space heater.

With the space heater, you can provide a decent amount of heat to keep the interior warm and comfortable. However, you can only do this with a regular heater when you're present in the RV.

These devices function like regular space heaters but offer some unique features. The smart space heaters are:

- Programmable.
- Operate automatically.
- Controllable via your smartphone.

Being programmable allows you to set up a schedule for when the heater should come on and go off, regardless of your presence in the home. In many cases, the devices are also preset to automatically come on when the temperature in the RV drops below a certain level and turns off at a specific temperature. With the option to control the space heaters with your smartphone, you can turn it on to start heating up as you make your way back to your RV.

Nested Cookware

You can also consider this as a storage tip for your RV living. Purchasing sets of nested cookware helps you save space in storage since you can stack each piece of the set. You must consider this when going to the store.

Mini Torch

There are different reasons you need a mini torch, which makes it an essential part of your RV-living. The torch helps start a fire, lights your candles, and starts a stove.

Instant Pot

The instant pot is another gadget you need in your RV. Many individuals will argue that the instant pot is unnecessary since most RVs have a kitchen setup. However, the time it takes to cook with an instant pot is less than what you need with the stove in your RV.

An instant pot helps you save time that you can use to engage in other activities. If you have a large family, you shouldn't overlook the importance of having an instant pot while traveling or living in your RV.

Folding Firepit

Firepits are essential in outdoor living and camping exercises. However, moving a metal firepit around can be inconvenient and even worse when you have to store it in your RV. To deal with this problem, you can shop around for a folding firepit.

These firepits are portable and easy to store. There are various types of firepits, and you can choose one based on its primary fuel source. Some firepits require wood, while others are gas-powered.

When making a choice, remember that while wood may be cheaper, you need to go through a lot of stress to use it. On the other hand, propane is faster and easier, and its use is not restricted by burn bans, which may occur in specific locations.

Foldable Luggage or Travel Bags

You should already notice a pattern with the gadgets mentioned here. When purchasing an item to go in your RV, first search for a foldable option. These foldable items help you save space on storage, an essential feature on RVs where storage space is limited.

Foldable luggage or travel bags may also offer multipurpose use. Some of these bags can serve as your suitcase and day pack. Hence, finding the right hybrid bag can save you money and space.

There are so many other gadgets that will come in handy during your RV living. These are some of the most essential, and you're sure to discover other valuable gadgets over time.

Some other gadgets that often come in handy include:

- Pop-up lanterns.
- LED rope lights.
- Anderson leveler.

- Water filtration system.
- Home theater.

My Favorite Spots Travel Guide

Not all destinations are equal. Many of it has to do with personal preference. Some people will enjoy lavish campgrounds with flashy amenities, while others will enjoy off-the-grid locations with access to greater wildlife and scenic views. I'll go over a few of my favorite spots. Some of these made the list because of the RV parks themselves, while others made it for their location and the activities the area had to offer.

- Yellowstone National Park – Located primarily in Wyoming. It's the flagship park for a reason. Beautiful scenery and a ton of great campgrounds to choose from no matter what your budget.
- Crater Lake National Park – Located in Klamath, Oregon. One of the most beautiful spots I ever had the privilege of visiting. The bluest water and incredible sheer cliffs. It was a sight to behold.
- Horse Thief Lake – A campground Located in Hill City, South Dakota, and one of my favorite spots to visit due to its proximity to both Custer Stater Park and Mt. Rushmore. This RV Park has lots of old-time charm. It offered shops for your basic supplies, as well as fire rings for each site and a heated pool.
- Blue Ridge Parkway – This is a huge park located in both Virginia and North Carolina. Tons of scenic vistas, mountain ranges, and old farmsteads make this an amazing place to visit and see for yourself.
- Durango RV Resort – This is an RV park in Red Bluff, California. In this campground, you'll find a lot of higher-end amenities. Every site has Powerhouse Pedestals. These are great for allowing you to have cable TV, electricity, and high-speed Wi-Fi. This RV resort also comes with pools, outdoor fireplaces, a nice clubhouse, and a dog park for your animals.
- Arches National Park – Located in Grand County, Utah. Arches is a beautiful park that holds over 2000 naturally preserved sandstone arches. There are tons of different landscapes and colors to take in when visiting this park.
- Rivers Edge RV Park – This Park is located in Fairbanks, Alaska. It offers gorgeous scenery and a ton of outdoor activities. These include hiking and biking trails, as well as fishing and hunting. They even offer shuttle buses into town so you can keep your RV hooked up at the campground.
- Grand Canyon National Park – Located in Mohave, Arizona. You need to travel to the Grand Canyon at least once in your lifetime. It's magnificent. I actually took a helicopter

ride through the Grand Canyon (we even landed in the Canyon and had lunch). We also went over to the Hoover Dam. Overall, it was an incredible experience.

- Boyd's Key West RV Park – Located in Key West, Florida. A great waterfront RV park that is right near town and all the fun Key West has to hold. The Park has both a pool and beach area. It even has its own marina. This is a popular spot among travelers, but well worth the trip.
- Fort Wilderness, Disney World — Located in Lake Buena Vista, Florida. They offer a nice campground if you ever want to visit Disney World without having to stay in a hotel. My family loved it here. They offer a bunch of amenities and activities, plus Disney World itself. Great for family vacations!

Commonly Asked Questions

What Is the Worst Thing About Living in an RV?

There is a lot of neat stuff about living in an RV, but unfortunately, there are also some major cons. No permanent address and the constant worry of being stranded can be a little bit stressful. On top of that, you're going to have to deal with hordes of other RVs on the road, which might be overwhelming for a newbie. For these reasons and more, it's good that we have some smart websites like Roadid that offer campsites to travelers all over the country for free.

What Is the Best Thing About RV Life?

No more mortgage, no more rent, no more long commutes. Say goodbye to neighborhood associations, lawns, and excessive landscaping. You can travel to new cities with a snap of your fingers or explore these amazing United States of America from coast to coast without paying for expensive flights or expensive hotels.

How Can You Do Laundry?

I've never visited an RV park without laundry services available. Many campgrounds offer this too. I once watched a moose, and her two babies walk by while I was washing clothes in Denali National Park. Larger RVs—Class A's and fifth wheels—may have a washer and dryer or a washer-dryer 2-in-1 unit built-in. You can also buy tiny little portable washers for your RV if public laundry options aren't your thing.

Do You Feel Safe on The Road?

I feel safer living on the road. I'm not worried about some random murderer jumping out from behind a door and attacking me; what keeps me awake at night is someone driving by my house and throwing a rock at my window.

Isn't Gas Mileage Terrible?

No, it's not. The average fuel efficiency of an RV is about 20 miles per gallon, which is considered pretty good for a car these days. If you take it easy on the gas pedal and avoid congested highways, you can get up to 30 miles per tank of gas. You should also know that RVs use diesel engines—even when they're running on gasoline - so that's one less downside to worry about!

When Will You Start Living a Normal Life Again?

There is no definite answer to this question, and it depends on your personal situation. There is usually some sort of "point" when one stops being in "RV mode" and starts living a more normal life. Sometimes this point will be brought about by an event such as a reunion with family or friends, which interferes with your ideal RV living plans.

Can You RV Full-Time in the Winter?

Yes! It's perfectly safe to live in an RV in the winter. The RV lifestyle is a great way to travel all year round without worrying about dreary weather or limited storage.

How Do You Stay in Shape While on the Road?

We had a Planet Fitness membership during our first year on the road because they have the most locations nationwide, and it's only $20/month to access all their gyms. Now we have our kayaks, a yoga mat, and hiking boots to keep us active!

Do You Get Tired of Living in a Small Space?

The most simple answer is no. I miss taking bubble baths on occasion, and I realize this may sound strange, but some people enjoy soaking in a tub. To me, baths are amazing, and I guess I can admit that I miss some of the tiny luxuries such as Wi-Fi and dishwashers every now and then.

But when talking about space, I haven't ever felt cramped or tired of living in a tiny space. Well, for the past six years that I've been living my life on the road, I have never felt cramped for space. As long as we keep the space clean and do the dishes after each meal, make our bed each morning, which helps make the RV feel a lot larger.

What Do You Do with the Poop?

Knowing how to handle waste is important as a hygiene-minded person who does not want to live in an unbearable stench of her own making. Even if it's for a short trip or just during the winter.

The simplest answer is: never let it build up. But what if there are times when this can't be done without help? At this point, patience is key—and using toilet paper as sparingly as possible when there's no running water nearby.

Do You Need a Special License to Drive a Motorhome?

For most rigs, no. It has to do with weight and state law. Likely, you won't have to worry about this. If you have a huge RV, google RV license requirements in your state.

How Do You Cook Meals?

Our rig has a three-burner stove and an oven big enough to fit a 13x9 pan. I can cook anything in our rig, including roasting a whole chicken, steaming vegetables, popping homemade popcorn, and making lots and lots of tacos. So far, the only thing I haven't mastered is chocolate chip cookies in the propane. I did make a killer funfetti cake for our anniversary, so it's time I give cookies another try. The key is to line the bottom of your pan with foil, so the flame of the propane oven doesn't crisp the bottom of your food!

Where Do You Stay When the RV Needs Service?

This is a HUGE concern for many people. Fortunately, there are many options.

- Most service shops will let you stay in the RV overnight in their lot. This has worked out for us 100% of the time so far.
- Your RV insurance may reimburse you if you need a hotel. During our first breakdown, it was 100° outside in Arizona, and our A/C couldn't keep up. We grabbed a hotel room (that luckily was right across the street so we could walk to it!) and sent the receipt to our RV insurance. (We found that insurance using Good Sam.)
- Put the RV in for service when you're flying out of town. We do this all the time and time, and it works out most of the time. You know your home is safe, and you don't have to worry about being kicked out from 9 AM to 5 PM every day. This works best when you're having multiple things done on the RV that might take days.

Conclusion

In the conclusion of this book, we talk about how to prepare for your RV living experience. Before committing to an RV lifestyle, you must mentally, physically, and financially prepare yourself.

#1: Prepare Your Mind

You must prepare your mind for RV living. You can do this by educating yourself, reading everything you can get your hands on about the lifestyle and/or make sure that you've attended several RV/mobile home shows. Research some of the RV parks and park models out there, read reviews online and see which ones to avoid. Talk to other RVers and find out what worked for them and what didn't work for them before they even go into their first travel trailer or RV! Read the campground rules and make sure you understand what they're about before going into your second or third park! Make sure you practice good common sense when traveling in an RV. Always keep your nose clean and obey the traffic laws. Be a good neighbor in all the places you travel through, and make sure you're ready for whatever life throws at you. You must also be ready to deal with emergencies and know how to deal with stressful situations. Practice having good emotional control, and get a little peace of mind by packing your supplies properly beforehand so that you're never caught off guard.

#2: Prepare Your Body

You must train your body to withstand the rigors and hardships of nomadism. This entails taking care of your health and eating habits. The simplest way to accomplish this is to plan ahead of time what type of food you'll eat, where you'll shop, how much money you'll spend shopping, and so on. Also, don't forget that you'll need to exercise regularly if you expect to enjoy and even thrive in this lifestyle. Make sure to take care of your health before entering into a travel trailer lifestyle.

#3: Prepare Your Finances

Even if you don't intend to buy an RV right away, it's critical to have enough money saved up for your first few months of living in one. You want to be sure you can pay rent at the RV park and buy food, water, and other necessities without running out of cash. If you don't save this money, you'll find yourself in a situation where you need money but can't get it until your finances improve.

#4: Prepare Your Time

You must realize that an RV lifestyle requires a lot of your time. You need to make sure that you have enough time to do what you want to do and have a relaxed life. If you don't plan ahead of time, chances are you'll end up wasting a lot of time on tasks that won't benefit you in the long run. Ascertain that this is not a problem for you!

#5: Prepare Your Life Partner—Marriage or Cohabitation

It would be beneficial if you were certain that you are prepared for the rigors of RV life, as well as prepared for your partner's reaction to this lifestyle. If you're currently married or living with someone, then you probably need to understand that your partner doesn't need to go along with you into an RV lifestyle. There is a high chance that they will want a change in their lives and may not handle it. This will also come into play if you're single—do you have the money situation set up before getting started? You will not likely find love while traveling in a trailer!

Made in the USA
Middletown, DE
16 December 2023

45990054R00091